David Fontana is currently Distinguished Visiting Fellow at the University of Wales, Cardiff, and holds professorships at the universities of Algarve and of Minho in Portugal. He is the author of numerous research publications and of twenty books which have been translated into twenty-two languages. For many years he has studied the relationship between Western and Eastern psychological systems, together with methods for deepening and expanding consciousness, and has written widely on dreams, meditation and psychospirituality. As well as being a meditator of many years standing and the father of two grown-up children, he is a Chartered Psychologist, a Chartered Counselling Psychologist, and a Fellow of the British Psychological Society.

Ingrid Slack holds a first-class degree in psychology and is a qualified and experienced teacher of young children. Currently she is a course manager with the Psychology Department of the Open University in Britain, and she also has worked as a consultant for and presenter of Open University television programmes. She is a Chartered Counselling Psychologist and has a long-standing interest in meditation and personal growth.

Also by David Fontana

Space in Mind
The Elements of Meditation
The Meditator's Handbook
The Secret Power of Dreams
The Lotus in the City
Know Who You Are: Be What You Want
Growing Together: Parent–Child Relationships as a
Path to Wholeness and Happiness

Also by Ingrid Slack

Learning and Conditioning

Teaching
Meditation
to Children

A PRACTICAL GUIDE TO
THE USE AND BENEFITS OF
MEDITATION TECHNIQUES

David Fontana
and
Ingrid Slack

E L E M E N T

Shaftesbury, Dorset • Rockport, Massachusetts
Melbourne, Victoria

First published in Great Britain in 1997 by
Element Books Limited
Shaftesbury, Dorset SP7 8BP

Published in the USA in 1998 by
Element Books, Inc.
PO Box 830, Rockport, MA 01966

Published in Australia in 1997 by
Element Books and distributed
by Penguin Books Australia Ltd
487 Maroondah Highway, Ringwood,
Victoria 3134

Cover design by Slatter-Anderson
Page design by Roger Lightfoot
Typeset by Bournemouth Colour Press
Printed and bound in Great Britain by Creative Print & Design, Wales

British Library Cataloguing in Publication data available

Library of Congress Cataloging in Publication data
Fontana, David.
    Teaching Meditating to children: a practical guide to the use and
  benefits of meditation techniques / David Fontana and Ingrid Slack.
        p.   cm.
    Includes bibliographical references and index.
    ISBN 1–86204–018–4 (pbk. : alk. paper)
    1. Meditation–Psychology. 2. Children–Religious life.
I. Slack, Ingrid. II. Title.
BL627.F656   1997
158.1'2'083—dc21   97–26610
                                              CIP

ISBN 1 86204 018 4

This book is dedicated to all children and to the adults who love and care for them, in the hope that it will help them to enjoy peaceful and fulfilling lives.

Contents

Acknowledgements

We would like to thank all the adults and children who have worked with us in meditation, particularly those who have let us quote their cases here. A special thank you goes to the staff and pupils in Kent's Hill First School in Milton Keynes for their co-operation, flexibility and support.

Introduction

This book is for adults, and explains how to introduce children to meditation. The idea of teaching meditation to children is relatively new to the Western world, but in the East meditation has long been accepted as an essential part of early education, laying down skills which are of lifelong benefit.

The book is intended for all adults who wish to teach meditation to children. That includes parents, school-teachers, youth leaders, social workers, psychologists, church workers, grandparents, uncles and aunts, and anyone who has contact with children in an official capacity and who wishes to help them make the best use of their extraordinary minds. This book is based upon our own experience as psychologists who have worked extensively with children, and who have written about and taught meditation to all age groups.

Children are impressionable human beings, and very much open to direction and influence by adults. Thus any attempt to introduce them to meditation must be done sensitively and wisely (we have more to say about this in Chapter 2), and must empower them not only to meditate, but also to judge the usefulness of meditation for themselves. This ability to judge will allow them to decide whether or not meditation is right for them. Of all activities, meditation is perhaps the one where success most depends upon voluntary participation. In addition, as meditation involves working with one's own mind, children should be given the right to accept or reject it as they think fit.

This book is intended to help you to introduce children to

meditation easily and effectively, and in the right spirit. It is not intended to be prescriptive; it provides a range of techniques and skills from which you are free to choose the ones most appropriate to your own children and your own circumstances.

In most cases in the following pages we talk about children as a group, but most of what we say applies equally well to parents and others who may be working with only one child. As already indicated, the book is intended just as much for parents – either both or just one – as it is for teachers working with larger numbers.

There are three overall objectives which we have kept firmly in mind throughout our writing. Essentially, we hope the book will explain the value of teaching meditation to children, provide the background knowledge necessary to work with children from around seven years of age through to the late teens, and give a range of practical exercises from which the reader can select in order to carry out this teaching. Not all the exercises are suitable for all situations. What works well with a small group of children may not be practical with a large class. You are the best judge of when to use the exercises as they stand, and when to adapt them in one way or another to suit the context within which you are working. The age of your children is another important variable, and we have more to say about this shortly.

We discuss the qualities needed by a meditation teacher in Chapter 2, but the one we must mention right at the outset is an interest in and a caring and sympathetic liking for children. No one who lacks these qualities can successfully teach children, whether the subject is meditation or mathematics or anything else. A good teacher works with children rather than dictates to them, and knows that a helpful and sensitive awareness of their needs and of their vulnerabilities brings success where hard words and grim authority all too often fail. The good teacher also knows that it is not enough merely to teach a child something. The child should be allowed to love what is being learned. In this way, lifelong interest can be built up, and the child helped to understand and appreciate the value of what is being learned.

We hope that nowhere do we make it seem that teaching meditation requires a great effort from the teacher. In fact, meditation is one of the most delightful of all subjects to teach. Whether working with children or adults, it is very rewarding to see a group of people find stillness and peace within themselves, and return to the challenges, difficulties and joys of life with renewed energy and enthusiasm.

We hope you enjoy teaching meditation to children. If you do, there is every chance that your children will enjoy learning from you.

A WORD OF WARNING

In view of children's impressionable nature, there is a natural concern among parents and teachers that they should not be indoctrinated with anything that smacks, however vaguely, of a cult of some kind. Indoctrination involves convincing people to believe something without giving them the tools to appraise it for themselves, and reject it if they think fit. Meditation isn't a cult, and doesn't belong exclusively to any one religion or philosophy. From time to time in this book there are references to the Buddha and to Buddhism, but this is only because the Buddha was the first person to try systematically to explain the theory and practice behind meditation. This book is not an apology for Buddhism, any more than it is an apology for any other belief system.

Unless you and your children are operating within a recognized and agreed religious framework (e.g. within a church or a denominational school), it is important that you teach meditation without the trappings of any particular set of beliefs, and without the kind of vague thinking that gets generally classified as New Age. Many parents will immediately object if they think their children are being introduced to ways of thinking of which they themselves may disapprove. Some meditation exercises for children which you may come across are grounded in very doubtful science.

For example, they might instruct the meditator to direct 'streams of light' to trees and flowers, or to 'send energy from one child to another'. These exercises are written by sincere men and women, but we live in a world where many people regard the ways of thinking upon which they are based as at best a waste of time, and at worst as actively misleading. So these somewhat esoteric approaches are best avoided until meditators are old enough and experienced enough to make personal decisions as to their value.

There is admittedly rather a fine line between encouraging children to use their visual imagination, and taking them off on flights of meaningless fantasy. But the line has to be observed, in fairness both to your children and to their parents. If you are working within a school, you will probably need the approval of the headteacher and perhaps also of parents if you are using anything more than simple meditations for physical relaxation. Such approval is rarely difficult to obtain, provided you set out clearly what your objectives are, and what meditation practices you intend to use.

CHILDREN'S AGES

The term 'children' is used throughout this book for all young people under the age of eighteen, which marks the transition into adulthood. Some people may find this strange. It is a sign of the hectic, frantic modern world that the term 'children' is coming to have a pejorative tone to it, and is beginning to be dropped in favour of such absurdities as 'school students' for children as young as five. We take the view that childhood is something to be honoured, and is as important a period of life as any other, so we are not afraid of the term.

This book provides material for use with children from as young as five right through to eighteen. However, although the basic techniques we present are the same for all ages, the way in which these techniques are presented, and the details they contain, will inevitably differ in some cases. We give guidance on this wherever it is really necessary, but it would be tedious to give every exercise in a different form for each age group of children. Accordingly, you may find the need to adapt individual exercises to suit the stage of development your children have reached. This isn't difficult to do, and the better you know your children, the easier you will find it to be.

We give more details about children and their needs and abilities in Chapter 2 and from time to time throughout the book, but there are, however, certain preliminary guidelines to bear in mind, and the most important of these are summarized below.

Five- to eight-year-olds

Children of this age find abstract thinking usually beyond them, and need to have everything related in some way to the practical experiences they have already had in life, i.e. to the things they have seen and heard and touched. They have vivid powers of imagination, but these powers do not extend to anything which lies beyond these practical experiences. Nevertheless, television and videos have exposed them to far more of these experiences than was the case even a few years ago, and the range of stimuli and of examples that you can use in your meditation exercises is more than extensive enough.

The second point to remember about this age group is the children's love of stories, rhymes and songs. Simple exercises like reading a story aloud, or singing a song together, and then asking them to close their eyes and imagine the characters and the actions they have just been hearing about are an invaluable preparation for meditation. They also help lengthen children's attention span and develop the depth of their interest, points to which we shall return in detail later.

Nine- to twelve-year-olds

This age group spans the junior school years and the beginning of high school. During these years children mature rapidly, and their interests, general knowledge, and powers of thinking and reasoning all develop considerably. For the most part, however, they still need to have new material linked clearly to things they have already experienced, and abstract concepts still present some difficulty.

Children of this age still enjoy stories, and their imagination remains as vivid as ever, provided that it has been encouraged and not dismissed by adults as immature daydreaming, but they now begin to show an overriding desire to be interactive. They want to initiate activities, to take responsibilities, to have a say in how things are said and done, to have questions answered, to receive explanations, and to discuss, question, debate and argue. Little progress will be made by the adult who simply tells them what exercises they are to do, and expects them to get on with them passively.

Thirteen- to fourteen-year-olds

Children show marked changes in their behaviour during their early high school years. There is a tendency to turn away from anything that appears in any way childish, and to assert more and more their independence from adult authority. The peer group becomes of increasing importance, and it is difficult for teachers to hold the attention of anyone whose friends reject the activity concerned.

During these years, most children become capable of abstract thinking, which not only extends the scope of the meditation exercises that can be used, but also allows them to discuss more deeply many of the concepts associated with meditation. Compassion, empathy, universal love, wholeness, tranquillity, peace, concentration, mindfulness (attentiveness), spirituality, spaciousness, eternity, beauty, truth, openness, purity and so on can all now enter freely into the language you use, and children can see that meditation is not only a way of having a gentle and relaxing inner experience, it is also a way of reaching out towards people and things, and arriving at a deeper sense of harmony and unity with the rest of creation.

Later adolescence

The ages fifteen to eighteen inclusive mark the final stage of the transition from childhood to adulthood. Although still limited by their inadequate experience of the world, children in late adolescence are in many ways physically and intellectually the equals of their parents and teachers. They need to understand the things they are doing, and to recognize that they are of value not only now but for the future as well. If they are to take more than a passing interest in meditation, they should be helped to see it as a practical skill for life, something that will help them become more effective as well as more balanced and sane human beings.

It is often harder to introduce the theory and practice of meditation to children of this age group than to any other. They tend to be naturally critical of anything to which adults try to introduce them, preferring to see for themselves what is on offer, and to make their own choices. This is discussed in more depth in Chapter 15.

No matter what their age, all children like to succeed. It is little use trying to teach through failure. Always concentrate upon teaching through success. Find a level at which children can get things right, and then move gently and at the right speed upwards from there. If children fail at something they will, dependent upon temperament and upbringing, either blame themselves for a lack of ability, or reject the whole thing as not worth doing anyway. Avoid this by always working at the appropriate level. Two or three minutes of effective and enjoyable meditation are worth far more than double or treble this time spent in frustration and boredom.

Nobody need fail at meditation. Meditation is a natural state of the mind, the state to which it automatically returns when we stop bombarding it with mental chatter. Under no circumstances allow children to make a bad start at experiencing this natural and enjoyable state.

RAISING AWARENESS

Although the techniques of meditation, at least at the level at which we are discussing them, appear relatively simple, meditation itself covers a vast area of human psychology. Thus, although the title of the book refers only to meditation, we have much to say about the raising of children's awareness – awareness of their minds, of their bodies, of the outer world, of their imagination, and of their thoughts and feelings.

In addition we have much to say about the problems children encounter in their psychological lives, the reasons for these problems, and the way in which meditation can help children deal with them. We do not see meditation as an esoteric practice designed to take the meditator away from everyday life, but as a peerless system of mind training and self-exploration that renders children more effective in what they do. As we explain in the following pages, meditation can enhance children's learning, memory, self-awareness, emotional balance, powers of attention, creativity – and above all their sense of inner harmony and peace. Meditation will not suddenly turn children into different people, but it has the potential to make them much better at being all the good things that they really are.

THE STRUCTURE OF THE BOOK

This book explores chapter by chapter the range of abilities with which meditation can be of help to children. Part 1 explains the rationale behind teaching meditation, while

Part 2 covers the different areas of life which can be enhanced by meditation. You will find explanations of the most suitable meditation techniques, practical exercises for introducing these techniques to children, and a range of other exercises which support meditation and help develop the necessary mental attitudes. You will also find the theory that allows you to render meditation fully understandable and, we hope, acceptable both to you and to your children.

The last section of this book discusses the practicalities of introducing meditation to children, whether you are working with small groups, with a whole class of children in school, or with your own children at home. These chapters cover such things as the organization of space, the links between meditation and the rest of the school timetable, and methods for gaining and holding the children's interest. We illustrate the advice given in these chapters by referring back to the basic exercises with which any programme of meditation with children should commence.

It is suggested that you read right through the book before beginning your work. In this way you will have a thorough knowledge not only of the material with which you will be dealing, but also of some of the problems you may encounter on the way.

PART 1

Meditation and Children

Chapter 1

Why Meditation?

Many of those reading this book will already have some experience of the benefits of meditation, and be more concerned with how to use it successfully with children than with explanations of its nature and value. However, others will be new to the subject, and will want some background. Even those who meditate regularly may welcome the opportunity to have certain of the fundamentals re-emphasized.

The details of meditation are set out fully in two earlier books, *The Elements of Meditation*, and *The Meditator's Handbook*, written by one of the present authors. But the term is used in a variety of different and potentially confusing ways, so let's start by looking briefly at what meditation is not.

WHAT MEDITATION IS NOT

One of the most common misunderstandings about meditation is that it is a kind of daydreaming, a process in which the mind is allowed to follow flights of fancy or idly play with ideas. Almost as common is the belief that listening to music or focusing upon the associations set up by a theme such as peace is meditation. Another mistake is to see meditation as a kind of trance, comparable in some ways to a hypnotic trance, or as deep relaxation in which the mind experiences tranquil thoughts or happy memories, or visualizes pleasant scenery or imagines itself floating in the air or drifting on bright water.

Each of the above states has its own benefits at appropriate times, but none of them is meditation. In each of them, the mind is occupied by thinking, or enjoying a sleepy or dreamy condition in which there is no particular clarity of focus. Such activities are very different from meditation.

A mistake of a different kind is to see meditation as a determined struggle to 'stop thinking', and by a supreme effort of will to keep the mind a blank sheet upon which nothing is allowed to be written. Equally misguided is the attempt to occupy the mind so fiercely with a mantra (a repeated word or phrase, about which more later) that it has no space for anything else. Activities of this kind restrict the mind rather than allow it gradually to expand into a richer and deeper dimension, and lead to boredom and frustration. The mind soon tires of the effort involved, and becomes increasingly irritated with the fact that no matter how hard one tries, thoughts still succeed in breaking through into consciousness.

WHAT MEDITATION IS

Meditation is not just about sitting in quiet concentration, central as this is to the practice. It is also about a range of active techniques that enhance the powers of mind control used not only while this sitting is taking place, but also in the rest of waking (and perhaps even of dreaming) life. Meditation thus touches most aspects of human experience, rendering them potentially richer, profounder and more meaningful.

In one form or another, meditation has been practised by all the great spiritual traditions, and its origins are lost in the mists of time. It is almost certain that the authors of the Hindu Vedas, which date from around 1,500 BCE and constitute some of the oldest scriptures in the world, practised meditation. Some of the earliest teachings on the basic technique of meditation (watching the breath, of which much more later) were given orally by the Buddha around 500 BCE. Patanjali, the semi-legendary founder of yoga philosophy, provides even more details in the Yoga Sutras, which date from the second century BCE. An unbroken tradition of meditation extends from Patanjali down to the present day, when probably more people meditate worldwide than ever before.

Meditation is essentially a state of poised, highly directed concentration, focused not upon a train of thoughts or ideas, but upon a single, clearly defined stimulus. Meditation is the very opposite of wandering thoughts or even of a directed train of thinking. A fifth-century Buddhist monk, Buddhaghosa, spoke of meditation as a *training of attention*. Other early writers have referred to it more broadly as a training of the mind, or as a way of understanding what is going on within the mind. Over the years, yet other writers have defined meditation variously as stilling the mind, as focusing mental energy, as discovering the true self, as achieving inner peace, as harmonizing body and mind, or simply as as sitting quietly, doing nothing. But it is a very special kind of sitting quietly doing nothing, in which the mind is held clear and still, alert and watchful, and free from losing itself in thinking.

Phrases such as training the mind come as something of a surprise to many Westerners. Isn't our formal education system, in schools and in universities, a training of the mind? Isn't the mind trained by learning the facts and figures and techniques of the various academic subjects that are taught by our teachers and our lecturers? Why should we need to bother with something as apparently esoteric and time-wasting as meditation?

Unfortunately, the mind quite categorically is not trained by the facts and figures and techniques that are taught in our school and university years. The knowledge we gain during these years is of enormous value to us and in many cases to our fellow men and women, but it does not constitute a training of the mind. Those who doubt this statement might like to try a simple little test. Close your eyes and stop thinking . . . How did you get on? Very few people can manage such an apparently simple task for even half a minute. So who is in charge of your mind? One thing is certain – if you can't stop thinking even for thirty seconds, it certainly isn't you.

We tend to suppose that 'thinking' is a good thing. So indeed it is, provided we have some power over the way in which thoughts arise and the direction which they take. However, for much of the time we have neither. Thoughts arise involuntarily and unbidden, and set off typically on their own course, with associations giving rise to each other in the manner of a rollercoaster. Happy thoughts, sad thoughts, anxieties, memories, hopes for the future, and regrets for the present and for the past – each of them goes its own way and exerts its own power over us. The same is true of feelings and emotions, which can carry us away like leaves caught in the wind.

A Zen Buddhist master, near the end of his life and in physical pain, once smiled at his disciple and asked, 'Have you yet realized that thought is the enemy?' Of course, thought is not always the enemy. Much depends upon our ability to think our way through problems, and to create our poetry and our science and our drama and our arts. But thought can often be the enemy, when it dominates our inner life instead of allowing us to be the masters.

The question sometimes arises, do we exist when we are not thinking? Such a question indicates the questioner's lack not only of control over his or her thinking, but a lack of any true self-knowledge. Of course we exist when we are not thinking, and until we have learned to demonstrate the fact for ourselves, we are little more than beginners in what we might call the art of being ourselves.

A mistake too often made is to equate this art with intelligence. The more intelligent we are, we are led to assume, the more we know ourselves and are in command of ourselves. Sadly or happily, depending upon your opinion of intelligence, this is far from the truth. Highly intelligent people are little better at running their inner lives than the rest of the human race. They may be better at solving certain kinds of problems in the outer world, but when it comes to solving those of the mind, their intelligence gives them few advantages.

The truth is that the mind isn't trained through knowledge and thinking. A university professor is not necessarily any better (and may often be far worse) at controlling his or her mind than someone who has had very little formal education. Knowledge and thinking allow the mind to be very good at handling the outside world, but they may be of little value in helping us to control what goes on inside our own heads.

The great majority of people who consult psychologists and psychiatrists with problems such as depression, anxiety, and stress, recognize that most of their difficulties come from thoughts which dominate, obsess or in other ways trouble their minds. Even though they may know that these thoughts are unhelpful and often untrue and actively counter-productive, they can do nothing to stop their incessant flow. Frequently people will confess that they know how damaging and unwanted their thoughts are, but they cannot do anything to put a stop to them and allow the mind to turn to happier and more productive ways of thinking.

In the East, one of the symbols of the mind is a chattering monkey, constantly producing noise but saying little of value. Another symbol is a runaway horse, totally out of control and ignoring the best efforts of the rider to tame it and turn it in the right direction. Symbols such as a chattering monkey and a runaway horse can help build up our motivation to practise meditation. Few people would willingly put themselves at the mercy of a chattering monkey or a runaway horse.

THE BENEFITS OF MEDITATION

What are the benefits of the mind training developed through meditation? They can be summarized as follows.

- *Physical relaxation* – meditation, as we shall see in due course, involves a letting go, a progressive ability gently to relinquish physical and mental tension. But it is also relaxation of an especially beneficial kind, involving a poised alertness which ensures that the body uses just the right amount of energy, not only to sit upright during meditation itself, but to carry out its daily physical tasks. Meditation in other words re-educates the body out of the bad habits of physical tension and unnecessary over-exertion that we pick up all too early in life. Together with this comes greater body awareness. The meditator is in effect tuned in to his or her body, so that tension is noticed and relaxed.

- *Improved concentration* – concentration is the foundation upon which all meditation systems rest. We have so much to say about concentration throughout the book that we don't need to elaborate further here. But not only is meditation built upon concentration, it is also one of the very best ways of *developing* concentration. And concentration developed in meditation, because it is pure concentration rather than the ability simply to concentrate upon something that captures the interest, quickly generalizes to other areas of life. The meditator is thus better able to turn his or her mind to whatever needs learning or doing, and focus upon it until the task is completed.

- *More control over thought processes* – this does not mean that the meditator can necessarily stop unwanted thoughts at will (although some meditators can). But it does mean that the meditator is less dominated by them. Put simply, he or she is aware of thoughts and observes them, but without being side-tracked by them. Unwelcome thoughts thus have less power to preoccupy or disturb the mind.

- *Increased tranquillity and the ability to deal with stress* – just as thoughts have less power to dominate the meditator, so have the emotions. The meditator may be aware of sadness or anger, but as with unwanted thoughts, these emotions are distanced from the meditator, who feels an inner peace and tranquillity in spite of them.

- *Improved mindfulness* – mindfulness is the ability to be aware of what is happening around us, and to turn our attention from one thing to another as it makes its appearance, rather than being so lost in distracting inner thoughts and dialogues that we go through life as if in a waking dream.
- *Enhanced self-understanding* – if we were asked if we knew ourselves, the answer would usually be yes. But in fact most of us are strangers within our own minds. We tend to live on the surface of our inner lives, aware only of conscious thoughts, and oblivious of what happens in the deeper levels of the unconscious. We are even ignorant of how our thoughts arise, or from where they actually come.
- *Improvements in creative thinking* – creativity involves accessing, or opening up to, the unconscious levels of the mind where original ideas are born. The quieter the conscious mind, the better able we are to reach these levels.
- *Improvements in memory* – much of our forgetting is due to our failure to concentrate upon what is happening, and thus to store it in our memory banks. Much more is due to interference by the conscious mind – particularly when we are worried or anxious, for example before sitting an examination or taking a test. Meditation helps to still these inhibiting emotions and allow us to recall the things we need. This is helped by the improved awareness mentioned above. We cannot hope to remember things effectively unless we are fully aware of them in the first place. All too often we accuse children of being in a dream, and of forgetting things we consider important. Part of the problem is that we spend so much time telling them to think that we shut off a large part of their awareness of the outside world.
- *Enhanced spiritual development* – one doesn't have to be religious or even interested in religion to find meditation of value. Yet meditation is inseparable from spiritual development in many of the world's great religious traditions. Nothing further need be said about this at the

moment, but for all meditators, no matter what their spiritual beliefs, meditation can lead to a new way of seeing the world, a way in which the inter-dependency of all things becomes a lived experience, and in which feelings of compassion and love for one's fellow creatures become an integral part of one's world view.

In addition to these psychological and spiritual benefits, meditation also brings benefits in terms of health. These vary from person to person, but can include lowered blood pressure, reduced heart rate, and the various other physiological benefits that arise from relaxation and from reduced levels of stress. Such benefits operate not just when one is meditating, but as one goes about daily life. Meditators generally find themselves calmer and less prone to anxiety and negative emotions, and better able to cope with the challenges and pressures of living. In addition, by composing the mind in meditation before undertaking stressful tasks, they are often able to carry them out with greater success and with less strain upon themselves.

Meditation isn't something that can only be done when sitting cross-legged on a cushion. You can meditate standing up, lying down or sitting in a chair. The state of your mind is far more important than the position of your body, though sitting upright with a straight back does help the concentration which is an essential part of meditation. And meditation isn't something that can only be done in the silence and privacy of one's own room. You can meditate practically anywhere – on a train, waiting for a bus, before going into a meeting or an interview – in fact at any otherwise idle moment.

Children, of course, don't suffer from high blood pressure or the heart problems that take all too high a toll of adults. But it may well be that the seeds of these and many other adult illnesses are sown in childhood. The more we can help children to be at peace with their own bodies, the better chance we have of helping them avoid these killers in later life.

Chapter 2

Why Meditation with Children?

WHY SHOULD YOUNG CHILDREN MEDITATE?

The traditional picture of childhood as a time of careless innocence, with long holidays and afternoons of high summer, set against a background of the intimate security of family and friends, has perhaps gone for ever. However, the notion that childhood is a relatively stress-free period compared with adult life lives on. Few notions could be further from the truth. One way of bringing this fact home is to recognize that young children inhabit a world similar in many ways to that experienced by adults in medieval times. With the exception of the privileged few, young children have no real rights regarding money or property. They are subject to arbitrary and often inconsistent and unjust rules and decisions made by their elders, and to summary punishments for offences they may not even be aware of having committed. They have no votes, no control over political or judicial processes, and little choice in how to spend the hours from nine to four. They also inhabit a world where violence in the form of bullying and intimidation can lurk around every corner. Whether they like it or not, they have to sit tests and examinations, prepared and assessed by examiners they have never met, on which their future and their self-image crucially depend.

In addition to recognizing the powerlessness which society imposes upon the young, we must remember that children experience feelings, such as love, joy, fear, disappointment and anger, with an intensity which they may never match in adult life. Success or failure in intimate friendships and relationships may be more crucial to them, and peer group acceptance may count for more, than at any time in the future. In addition, the early years are a highly formative episode in the individual's life history. During these years the young not only have to learn the facts and figures demanded by a formal education, but also need to explore psychological and social issues to do with self-consciousness, personal identity, moral behaviour and the vast range of issues which go to make up community living.

Recognizing the nature and and strength of these pressures allows us to appreciate that stress, neuroses, unhappiness and depression are by no means the prerogative of adults. As psychologists and counsellors who have worked extensively with both children and adults, we have found the same range of symptoms and difficulties among individuals of all ages. The only real difference is that young children find it harder to articulate their problems, and to be taken seriously, than do their elders. All too often children suffer in silence, incurring psychological wounds that remain with them throughout their life.

Two examples help to illustrate this. Shirley,* who was sent away to school when a child, recently came across the bundle of letters she had written home to her mother, and was amazed that they contained no word of the almost permanent sadness she had felt during those years. 'The letters were full of chatty things about what we'd had for lunch, or about occasional outings into town, or our games lessons, or things my friends told me. There was nothing about my homesickness, my unpopularity with some of the teachers, my loneliness, and the fact that sometimes I actually wished I was dead.' Philip, who had just been watching a cine film of himself as a boy, couldn't identify at all with the happy, smiling youngster he appeared to be. 'I

---

*In order to protect anonymity some of the names and details in the case studies have been changed.

just don't know where any of that came from. I spent most
of my time scared of my parents, scared of bullying at school,
scared of getting poor marks, scared of being ill, even scared
of the dark. I hated being a kid.'

Even children with ideal family backgrounds and enviable
school experiences still suffer from physical and
psychological tensions in an ever more demanding
and stressful world. Unhappily, little is done within formal
education to help them learn to understand themselves, to
control their anxieties and their thought processes, and
to discover tranquillity, harmony and balance within
themselves. Little is done to help them to manage their own
inner lives, to use their mental energy productively instead of
dissipating it in worries and random thinking, and to access
the creative levels of their own minds.

Meditation is one of the most important ways in which we
can help young children cope better with their lives, at both
the personal and the academic levels. As we shall stress
throughout the book, meditation gives even very young
children power over their thinking and their emotions, not by
a repressive self-control, but by enhanced self-understanding
and self-acceptance. Meditation cannot make an unhappy
child happy overnight, or make up for all the deprivations
that some children suffer at the hands of their elders, but it
can lead towards greater happiness and enhanced self-
management.

WHY SHOULD ADOLESCENTS MEDITATE?

Much of what we said about young children applies equally
to adolescents. However, these older children have additional
problems of their own, and introducing them to meditation
can be more challenging than meditating with younger
children. A few brief additional background details about
this age group are therefore essential for those who plan to
start work with them.

After the first seven or eight years, adolescence is often the major formative period of life. By this time, children have learned what it is to be children, and to relate to the world as children do; now suddenly they have to learn to be adults, and to relate to the world as adults. In a very few short years, children go from physical childhood to physical maturity. They experience puberty, with the uprush of sexual energy and sexual desires that go with it (boys, in particular, characteristically reach their sexual peak between the ages of sixteen and eighteen). And with puberty comes a range of other powerful emotions. Hopes and disappointments are felt with a keenness comparable to that of early childhood, yet the adolescent is expected to exercise the self-control of an adult. The hormonal changes that help convert the adolescent body from that of a child into that of an adult contribute to a wild uprush of feelings, and to extreme mood swings that can often be as surprising and as worrying to the child as they are to his or her family and friends.

At adolescence, nature is preparing children for independence and freedom of choice. In myths, legends and fairy stories, puberty is the time when the young set out into the world to seek their fortunes. At this time a restlessness fills them, a powerful longing for something which they cannot readily put into words, a desire to leave the comfort of family and the familiar, and to seek new worlds and new experiences. Along with this goes a desire to reject the ideas and beliefs among which they have been reared, in order to experience the freedom of thought that goes with physical freedom. Capable now of abstract ideas as well as of physical and sexual self-assertion, they question, argue, debate, storm out of rooms, slam doors, enjoy loud music and loud disputes, upset the neat conformity of bedrooms and living rooms, rebel against rules, and often show an ill-disguised contempt for the quaint ways and opinions of their elders.

In place of these ways and opinions, the adolescent comes to rely increasingly upon the peer group. The peer group is now the arbiter of taste and of fashion, and to be accepted and liked by the group assumes monumental importance. Only through this acceptance is the child able to accept him- or herself. Acceptance by peers reassures the adolescent that he or she is managing life well, is making an acceptable transition from childhood, and will go on to be successful, admired and popular in adult life.

In cultures supposedly less civilized than our own, this acceptance comes not just from the peer group but from the whole of society. For both boys and girls, puberty is marked by initiation rites and ceremonies. The child is welcomed into adult life by the entire community. His or her development is recognized and celebrated. From that point the child becomes an adult, with the full rights, duties and responsibilities of the adult world.

In the West, we have no such initiations. Although physically mature, adolescents are still largely denied the full privileges and freedoms of adult life, with the result that, if they have spirit, they will fight hard for their rights. Friction between parents and children is more marked at this time than at any other. The young struggle for their freedom, and their elders struggle to keep them within the boundaries of childhood. At this time wise parents loosen the reins, knowing that the best way to keep their children is to let them go, and that if the foundations have been well laid in the early years, their offspring will make informed and sensible decisions for themselves.

However, due to a lack of education in mind training, most children, through no fault of their own, have developed bad mental habits by this age. Often their minds are a turmoil of excitements, hopes, expectations, anxieties and fantasies. The rate of depression among adolescents is typically high. Their mood swings lead to agonizing periods of self-doubt. Sometimes they even find it hard to recognize themselves in this new being who seems to be inhabiting their body. Virtually at no other time in life is there more need for a mind training that, without denying or seeking to judge or repress a single feeling or emotion, can settle the individual into a calm and relaxed state. Brian is a good example of how meditation can help.

Brian

Brian, in his early teens, found himself going through a dark period emotionally after the break-up of his parents' marriage. 'My main problem was that I didn't know *why* I felt so down. I missed our family life, but on the other hand my parents didn't get on well, and it was nice not to be hearing them rowing all the time. But each morning I woke up under this black cloud, which lasted most of the day, and began to interfere with my school work.' Meditation didn't cure Brian's depression immediately, but practising for a few minutes soon after waking helped him to look more objectively at his depression, instead of identifying with it. 'I saw that the depression was simply something that was there. It wasn't me; it was just something I was experiencing, and I was able to tell myself that like most things it wouldn't last.' Part of Brian's problem had been that he was depressed *about* being depressed, instead of seeing depression as a reaction to the sudden change in his home circumstances. Meditation helped him put things into perspective, and his natural good spirits soon began to re-assert themselves.

Adolescents who have been fortunate enough already to have had some experience of meditation often come increasingly to recognize its benefits. Even if they have not meditated for some years, they may now return to the practice of their own free will. The great Danish/American psychologist Erik Erikson considered that the prime task of adolescence is to discover a sense of identity, to answer at least in part the question 'who am I?' In meditation, the young person begins to see that there is something more to the self than the transitory, mood-changing, anxious, elated, fantasy-prone, sexually aroused individual who confronts the world each day. For him or her there is a tremendous sense of security in discovering a calm inner being with self-confidence and self-acceptance, who is not pulled this way and that by friends, family, teachers, and the confusion of personal emotions.

Adolescents who have had no training in meditation may

show a strong initial resistance to it. Adolescents want to be active, to be engaging with the world rather than sitting quietly watching their breathing. They are frequently lost in an inner dream state, but at such times may prefer to follow the ramblings of their own thoughts, rather than submit to a discipline practised and taught by an adult world which they have perhaps already written off as irrelevant.

However, there are ways of moving around this blockage. It is never a good thing to meet a spirited adolescent head-on. The more we insist on something, the more they will resist, not necessarily because they dislike what it is we are saying, but because it is we who say it. In consequence, when teaching meditation to this age group, it becomes more necessary than ever to start from a place where the children feel comfortable and have an interest. As we shall see in due course, we can use concentration exercises that use the image of an athlete or a pop star, or whoever it is who holds their attention. Once concentration becomes established, we can move on from there.

If the children with whom we are working have no background in meditation, it is important to start by talking a little about the value to *themselves* of developing their powers of concentration. The issue can be discussed with the group, and difficulties in maintaining concentration can be demonstrated by trying the experiment of attempting to stop thinking, as described on page 6. This consists simply in asking them to close their eyes, and to stop thinking for thirty seconds. (Remind them that repeating 'I'm not thinking, I'm not thinking' to themselves doesn't count!) At the conclusion of the exercise, discuss with the group why they found this difficult or impossible, and point out the lack of control they thus appear to have over what goes on inside their own minds.

The next step is to explain that their minds don't have to have these limits. The mind is the most powerful asset they have, and the more clear and focused it is, the more they can achieve in life, both personally, and in their work and in their relationships with others. Point out that to extend these limits, they need to be able to focus the mind upon one thing, without allowing it to wander off on a train of thought of its own.

YOUR OWN ROLE IN TEACHING MEDITATION

Should you be a meditator yourself in order to teach meditation to children? The short answer is – ideally, yes. If you are a meditator you will have had first-hand experience of some of the difficulties involved, and will also have something of the calmness of mind that comes with meditation, and that conveys itself to others. If you are interested in teaching meditation to children, the chances are, of course, that you will have been practising yourself, and are well aware of the benefits meditation can bring.

A teacher of advanced meditation practices must have had extensive personal experience, as difficulties can arise which can only be coped with by someone who has been in a similar situation. However, none of the techniques covered in this book fall into this advanced category, so even if you are new to meditation yourself, it is still possible for you to introduce it to children. The most important thing is your own mental attitude. Provided you are calm, sympathetic and supportive, and you keep to the guidelines we give throughout this book, most children will respond favourably. And you may well find yourself so influenced by your own teaching, that you become a meditator yourself almost without noticing it.

Remember that children, especially older children, are likely to ask whether you meditate. No matter what the subject, children like to feel that anyone who is teaching them has personally mastered and enjoyed the techniques concerned. However, whether you have had extensive experience or not, there are a number of simple preparatory rules that you should keep in mind when introducing meditation to children.

1 Don't expect too much. Some children take readily to

meditation, while others find it doesn't come so easily (though as we stress elsewhere, it's often the second group of children who have most need of the practice). Remember that many young children have a relatively short attention span. However much they enjoy meditation, they won't want to keep at it for long periods. We give more detailed guidance on this in Chapter 13.

2 Never show disappointment or impatience with your children. Remember that you are offering meditation to children, not forcing it upon them. In the final analysis, it is up to them whether they accept it or not. Impatience on the part of the teacher only makes learning harder for children. Bad learning experiences stay with children, and can put them off a particular subject for many years to come – sometimes for life. However much you love meditation yourself, and recognize its value for others, always keep in mind that if children don't want to embrace it, this is their choice. They may well return to it later on, provided you allow them to associate it with a generally happy, relaxed and pleasant atmosphere.

3 Make it clear children are not competing with each other. Children are given the impression early on in life that they are always being compared with each other when it comes to good work, stars, marks, housepoints, and even words of approval. Not surprisingly, they are likely to feel that comparisons of this kind are also being made during meditation sessions. They will wonder whether they are doing it as well as the other children, and may even try to vie with each other for your praise. Avoid this by making it clear at the outset that meditation, like breathing, is not an area in which we compete with each other. We can all meditate if we wish to do so. Reinforce this by taking care not to praise some children at the expense of the rest of the group. Keep praise general. And never be tempted to rebuke a child in front of the rest of the class. (Ways of dealing with uncooperative children are covered in Chapter 13.)

4 Keep all instructions simple. As stressed elsewhere in the

book, this is particularly important with younger children. Good meditation teachers use very few words when guiding their classes, because words can get in the way, leaving people thinking about meditation instead of actually doing it.

5 Keep explanations simple, again especially with younger children. Encourage discussion – it's always useful for children to know they can talk about their experiences – but remember that children will tend to try to outdo each other in their descriptions of what they have experienced. As soon as you see that fantasy is entering into their accounts, gently terminate the discussion, while assuring the class that they can return to it after the next meditation session. Once again, avoid encouraging any sense of competition between children; accept all their descriptions without praising some at the expense of others. If you have to point out that some of the accounts don't sound in the least bit like meditation, do it gently, and protect the child's fragile self-esteem. 'That's very understandable, but we need to go in a rather different direction' is much better than 'You've got the wrong idea; we'll have to go back to the beginning'.

6 Use an appropriate tone of voice. The voice should be gentle and quite soft, but not hypnotic or soporific. You don't want to send the group to sleep. (This is very easily done – we have had this experience even with adults.) Your words should be delivered confidently and without undue pauses, but should never be rushed. Meditation is a timeless business, and children should never be given the impression that it can be rushed.

Children learn best from adults they admire, and who provide them with a good example of the kind of person they themselves would one day like to become. If children see you as patient, caring, happy and relaxed (the qualities that meditation can help develop) they are far more likely to be motivated to practise than if they see you as exemplifying the very opposite qualities.

PART 2

The Practice of Meditating with Children

Chapter 3

Meditation for Mindfulness

THE MEANING OF MINDFULNESS

Concentration, and what is often referred to as mindfulness – which means an alert awareness of what is going on around one and inside one's own head – go very much together. Exercises in mindfulness help concentration, while the development of concentration in turn helps the development of mindfulness – and both help the memory, since children are much more likely to remember the things to which they have paid proper attention. There are a number of very enjoyable exercises that assist in the growth of mindfulness, and which therefore serve as an excellent preparation for the more intensive exercises in concentration that come later. In the present chapter, we give some of those most likely to appeal to children. But first, it is useful to help children recognize how fragmentary their memories are.

EXPLORING MEMORY

Much of the time children (and perhaps even more adults) fail to remember things because their minds are not focused upon what they are doing. It is important for children to become aware of this. Increased powers of attention, as we have already stressed, lead to greater effectiveness in learning and in most of the other things in which children engage, from sports to hobbies.

But there is another reason why an awareness of how poor our memories are is important to children, and it has to do once more with self-understanding. From an early age, children develop a belief that memory provides a complete record of our lives from day to day. This belief remains with us throughout life. We feel that our memories are our identity; that we are, in a sense, our memories. However, memory is an incredibly fragmentary thing. We remember – or we can access from our memories – only a minute fraction of all the things that happen to us.

This is no bad thing in a way. There is no point in remembering even the most trivial events. But children need to be made aware of how their memories work if they are not only to improve their recall of the important things, but also to understand that their real nature consists of more than just a series of disjointed fragments of past events.

Meditation 1: The Holes in Memory

This is a very simple and often very amusing exercise, and yet it can very quickly reveal to children the enormous gaps in their ability to remember the past. Introduce the exercise in the following way.

> I'd like you to think back to a day when you were enjoying yourself. Maybe it was a birthday, or a time when you were on holiday. Try to remember exactly how you felt when you woke in the morning, and what you did during the day. Go through as many details as you can – the things you said, the things people said to you, the clothes you wore, the objects you touched, the things you saw. Go right through to bedtime, and remember how you felt when the day was over.

The children should do the exercise in silence and with their eyes closed. Let it run for as long as you think the children are enjoying it. Many children will want to share their memories, and when they have done so, draw the attention of the group not to the things remembered, but to the things forgotten. What were the children doing *in between* the exciting events they have just been relating? Can they recall what they said, or what they were feeling? Make sure that they do not feel troubled by their inability to remember these less exciting details. The purpose of the exercise is to recognize this inability.

Follow-up

As a very short follow-up exercise, either at the same time or on a subsequent occasion, the children can be asked to recall what they were doing on the same day the previous week, or even on the previous day. Allow them to recognize that although they were awake for maybe two-thirds of the twenty-four hours, their memories of what happened may add up to only a few minutes. Point out that this is true for most days of their lives. Most of the pages of memory, and therefore of life, are blank when we turn back and try to look at them, so 'we' must be much more than our collection of memories.

If the children want to pursue things further, they can make a list of the things they remember from, for example, last year, and you can discuss with them why certain things are remembered, while all the rest are forgotten. Usually the events that are remembered have exciting or alarming associations, or were unusual in some way. Realizing this helps the children to see that, because of these emotional or novel qualities, special attention was given at the time to these experiences.

After trying this exercise, a lively class of nine-year-olds decided to try to improve their memories by keeping daily diaries of all the interesting things that happened to them. A few weeks later they suddenly agreed to collect all the diaries, shuffle them, and give them out at random. Each child then read aloud extracts from the diary he or she had been given in order to see how many of the class were able to recognize their own experiences. Once again, the children were surprised at how unreliable their memories sometimes proved to be.

Exercise 1: Kim's Game

Once the children have recognized the gaps in their memories, you can go on to the first memory exercise. This is known as 'Kim's Game' because of its appearance in Rudyard Kipling's novel *Kim*, the story of a young boy brought up in India who accompanies a Tibetan lama in his search for the fabled River of Immortality. Kim is taught many lessons in mind training during the course of the book, but this particular game is the most appropriate for the development of mindfulness. Although particularly suitable for use with younger children, who often learn best through play and through games, older children also enjoy and benefit greatly from it, as do many adolescents and even adults.

I [David] remember being taught Kim's Game years ago, soon after joining the Scout movement as a boy of eleven, and to this day I can recall the profound effect it had upon me. If I close my eyes, I can still see before me the tray with its many objects used in the game, and still relive the pleasurable effort to place each object into a slot in my memory. Kim's Game certainly sharpened both my awareness and my desire to look closely at things.

Kim's Game is an open-ended exercise, the difficulty of which can be varied, depending upon the age and the ability of the children. It is also profoundly simple to set up, fun to play, and capable of reaching deep into the way in which children look at the world. Each child will need a paper and pencil. (If very young children find difficulty in writing, they can play verbally instead.) You will need a timer or clock, a tray, and a range of everyday objects, as different from each other as possible. Examples of the kind of things you can use are given below.

Pencil, ruler, thimble, spoon, cup, apple, eraser, elastic band, paper clip, die, salt cellar, key, coin, audio tape, button, scissors, ink bottle, screwdriver, pen, computer disc, handkerchief, magnifying glass, ornament, diary, badge, necklace, marble, pine cone, letter, matchbox, flower, photograph, toothpaste, clothes brush, ribbon, fork, can opener, glove, knitting needle, stone, paintbrush, beads, eggcup, train ticket.

The list is virtually endless. Place the chosen objects on a tray, allowing sufficient space between each object for it to be clearly seen. Then leave the tray out of sight of the children while you explain the rules of the game. The children will be allowed to look at the tray for a given length of time. Then you will remove it and they will all be asked to write down (or remember and tell you) as many as possible of the objects they have just seen. They must not touch or move any of the objects, or talk to each other while the game is in progress. Stress that although it *is* a game, there are no winners and losers. You are only interested in each child enjoying the experience and doing his or her best.

There is no set time limit for studying the tray. In addition to the age and the ability of the children, much depends on the number and nature of the objects on the tray. The more objects and the more unusual they are, the longer the time needed. A good idea is to have one or two trial runs with children who are from a different group, but who are of approximately the same age and ability. Note how long you need to give them before they can get a reasonable number of objects correct, then give around seventy-five per cent of this time to the group with whom you are actually working. There is no set time limit for writing down either. The best rule of thumb is to watch the group and call a halt when everyone appears to be running out of ideas.

You will notice that after a few attempts at Kim's Game, the children improve rapidly. Some children work out a system (a so-called mnemonic device) of their own in order to aid their memories. For example, they may group all domestic objects together in their minds, and visualize them in the kitchen at home. Then they may group school objects such as pens and rulers together, and visualize them on their desk at school. Objects like ornaments and books they may visualize in their lounge at home, items of clothing in a cupboard, and beads and jewellery in one of the bedrooms. Other children may work on pure memory alone. The technique they use is not important. The purpose of the game is to train awareness. And provided the children are focusing on the objects in front of them, it matters little how they actually commit them to memory.

As the children improve at Kim's Game, it can be made correspondingly harder. Rudyard Kipling's young hero became remarkably proficient at it. However, it should never become anything other than fun for the children. If they begin to find it boring, discontinue it and move on. It will have served its purpose.

The purpose of the next two exercises, which follow on appropriately from Kim's Game, is to prompt children to realize how unmindful they are in normal daily life. Both exercises are particularly effective in bringing this realization home to them. If you are working with adolescents and have decided not to use Kim's Game with them, these two exercises are a good place at which to start.

Exercise 2: Mindfulness at Home

Children of all ages find this short exercise intriguing. Ask them to draw from memory the layout of their homes. In spite of the fact that their homes form the background to their lives, many children find it difficult to get the layout just right. An additional, or alternative exercise, would be to ask them to draw a map of the streets in their neighbourhood (with names), or even of their journey to school.

The difficulties frequently posed by these tasks help demonstrate to children the extent to which their minds are tuned to what we have called 'automatic pilot'. We often use terms like 'spatial awareness' or even 'spatial intelligence' in an attempt to explain why some children are much better at tasks like this than others. But the truth is that some children, like some adults, go through life with much more awareness than others. Many of the apparent differences between individuals arise not from differences in ability but from differences in the way in which ability is used.

This exercise can be repeated at a later date in order to note how much the children have improved. The next exercise is equally enjoyable – and equally revealing.

Exercise 3: Mindfulness in Daily Life

Provide the group with pencils and a plentiful supply of paper. Then ask them to draw in succession and from memory a number of everyday objects. You can choose the objects yourself, but the following list will give you some ideas.

> Lamp post, letter box, telephone, tree, bird, traffic bollard, road signs, chair, motor car, rose, shoe, bowl, table, vacuum cleaner, scissors, computer keyboard, doll, open book, audio tape, step ladders, human face, school desk, football, comb, spectacles, CD player.

Many of these objects are seen over and over again in the course of the average day, yet how accurately can the children reproduce them when asked to do so? The exercise isn't a test of skill at drawing, though inevitably children with proven artistic ability are likely to be more visually aware than most. It is a test of how much children notice as they go about their lives, of how mindful they are. Everyone has the ability to draw, and most children take great pleasure in doing so. The difference between those who do it well and those who do it less well is largely that the former take in more of what they see.

At the end of the drawing exercise, ask the children to select an ordinary household item from the list of objects they have just been trying to reproduce, and to take a good look at it when they get home. Ask them to study it from all angles, and to look at it several times before the next meditation session. Ask them not to try drawing it during this interim time (some of them will still do so, of course, but this does not really matter), but then to have another go at it when the next session takes place.

Their second attempts will usually be much more accurate than their first, but improvements in drawing skills are not the main point of the exercise. It is equally important that children be asked to discuss the reasons for these improvements. Help them to understand that the improvements do not arise merely from seeing the objects concerned. After all, they've been 'seen' on an almost daily basis over a long period of time, so frequency is not the secret. It isn't *quantity* of seeing that counts, it is *quality*.

And what is quality of seeing? And how does it differ from quantity of seeing? What is the difference between the way in which the children have now learned to take in the experience of seeing from the way in which they took it in before this learning took place? As with all question and answer work with children, don't be too ready to offer your own explanations. Allow the children to reflect and articulate for themselves. Something has happened between the first and the second attempt at the drawings. What is it, and why has it happened? And how can the children ensure that it goes on happening, not just with the objects they have been drawing, but with everything else they see around them?

A single experience of this quality of seeing can bring about a lasting change in the way in which children interact visually with the world. Once the children have been introduced to the art of *seeing*, with this exercise and with the exercise that follows on page 32, they will recognize how much they normally miss of the wonder and beauty of the world, and how for most of the time they take for granted the marvellous gift of sight instead of using it and appreciating it to its fullest extent.

A similar exercise can be carried out with tape recordings of common sounds, testing this time for the extent to which the children are mindful of aural experiences.

Robert, a ten-year-old who experienced some difficulty with much of his schoolwork, was particularly interested in each of the previous memory exercises, and proved highly successful at them, demonstrating yet again that many children's talents are often overlooked. His delight in his success was a pleasure to see, and there was a marked subsequent improvement in the confidence and commitment that he brought to bear upon the rest of his work.

THE FAMILIAR MADE UNFAMILIAR

An exercise used by art teachers to help develop a more complete and integrated way of looking at the world is to invite the children to draw familiar objects from an unfamiliar perspective. From childhood onwards we become so used to the appearance of objects that we frequently stop really seeing them. Not only does this create a sameness (and even a dreary staleness) about the way in which we see the world, it prevents us appreciating the unexpected beauty of form which many objects possess when we see them from unexpected angles.

At the philosophical level which some older children like to explore, seeing objects from a new angle raises questions as to their intrinsic nature. Much of our understanding of the world is based upon visual experience. Change that experience by altering the way in which things appear to us, and we recognize how subjective and ultimately 'illusory' our view of the world actually is. How different our concept of a commonplace object like a bottle is when it is turned on its side, and we view it only from the base. How different things look when they are upside down. How strange houses look when seen in an aerial photograph. How difficult it is to recognize someone's face when they are standing on their head. Come to that, how different the world looks when we stand on our own heads.

Exercise 4: Standing the World on its Head

Most children enjoy those puzzle pictures which present familiar objects from odd angles and ask you to identify them, so these ideas will not be entirely new to them. Provide the children with a photograph or painting of a familiar scene or a familiar object, turn it upside down, and ask them to draw it from this angle. Seeing and reproducing the picture in this unusual way will enable the children to relate to it as a series of interconnecting shapes, many of them with an intricacy and a beauty of form and line which are a pleasure to draw.

Ask the children not to turn their pictures the right way up until they are completed. When this is eventually done, the children will be interested to realize that not only have they had a new and captivating visual experience, but also they will often have produced far better drawings than they would had they reproduced the picture the usual way up. By getting away from concepts of how things should look, they will have simply drawn what is actually there, with results that are far more naturalistic and lifelike.

FORM AND SPACE

The next exercise completes the opening cycle of helping children to see the world more clearly, and to become more mindful of what they see. It also helps prepare them for the realization of the inter-dependency of all the objects around them, and of the fact that this inter-dependency extends to themselves as well. This realization is central to many of the meditation exercises that follow in subsequent chapters, and is indeed one of the most important insights into the ultimate nature of things that meditation can bring.

The visual world is made up of two classes of phenomena – material objects and empty space. Typically, we think of the world as defined by the first of these, yet in fact the second plays an equally important role. To demonstrate this, show the children a cup. Does its 'cupness' reside in the outer material form, or in the empty space which this form encloses? Help the children to appreciate that without both the form and the space, we would have no cup. Not only would we have no functional cup (you cannot pour liquid into it if there is no space to contain it), we would have no visual cup, as the form which encloses the empty space is itself defined by the space which surrounds it.

The final exercise of this chapter is suitable for all ages, and helps children to recognize that the visual world is in fact a pattern of interlocking shapes, some of them composed of form and others composed of space. Once this realization takes place, the world is likely to be seen in a much more wholistic and ultimately satisfying way. Teachers of drawing have long regarded this and similar exercises as essential in helping students view and conceptualize the world as a total visual experience.

Exercise 5: Form and Space

The children will each need paper and pencil for this exercise, and you will need to provide something for them to draw. It is better to use a scene (e.g. part of a room or a garden, or a view from a window) rather than just a few objects, as the more surfaces where form and space interlock with each other the better.

Ask the children to study the scene carefully, and explain that instead of drawing the outlines of the forms in front of them, they are to draw the outlines of the empty spaces between these forms. A little explanation and even a brief demonstration may be needed before they understand what you want them to do, but once they do understand, most children find it an intriguing challenge.

Allow the group as much time as they need for the drawing. When they have finished, you will probably be agreeably surprised by the quality of their work. By drawing spaces, which are essentially abstract in outline, the children will get away from their natural preoccupation with how the various solid objects in front of them 'ought' to look. Once they start thinking about this 'ought', their minds inevitably become caught up in conception (in ideas *about* objects) rather than in perception (in direct experience of how objects look). Drawing requires sensitivity to what is actually there, to the arrangement of pure shapes that make up our visual environment. By drawing these pure shapes, the children will find that, as if by magic, objects begin to appear on the paper in front of them.

Try this exercise yourself before giving it to the children. If you are not already an experienced artist, notice how your ability to draw becomes immediately enhanced. I [David] first tried it over a sustained two-week period some years ago, while camping in France and spending most of my time observing nature. Not only did my drawing improve, but at some point during the two weeks I experienced a sudden transformation in the way in which I saw the world. It was no longer composed of two opposites, form and emptiness, but of an enchanting pattern in which all phenomena were joined together in a dance of light and movement, shape and colour. The trees against the skyline seemed in love with the space around them, and were held by space in an embrace of joy. My own body was even part of this pattern, linked to space and through that space to the green and golden world of high summer. This feeling brought with it a wonderful sense of participating in a unity which not only created and sustained me, but which encompassed infinite dimensions of being.

Experiences of this kind typically come more easily to children than to adults. Children may not be able to articulate them, but the importance lies in the experience itself, rather than what they find to say about it. In work of this kind, never demand a verbal response from children if they find it difficult to give one. Children are usually anxious to please, and in the face of such a demand may fall back upon repeating the words of others, or saying what they believe you want to hear. Once inappropriate words are used to define an experience in this way, children tend to remember the words rather than the experience, and thus lose the essence of it.

In addition, by over-emphasizing words, we give children the impression that unless something can be talked about, it either does not exist or is of no importance. In fact many of the most profound experiences in life, from enjoying a sunset to gaining deep mystical insights, cannot accurately be expressed in words. Much the same applies to music and painting, which have a language of their own. You either understand the language or you don't. Asking the musician or the artist to explain their creations in words is to miss the point behind their inspiration.

REDISCOVERING MINDFULNESS

How often do we tell children to concentrate, or blame them for lack of concentration? Yet we do nothing to help them develop the ability to concentrate. It is a strange anomaly that children are all too frequently criticized for failing to show the behaviours that we most signally fail to teach them. How often are children blamed for not paying attention! 'Attention' thus becomes something of a dirty word for them, yet another of the sticks with which the adult world can beat them.

The exercises in this chapter are invaluable in teaching mindfulness skills – or rather in allowing our innate ability for mindfulness to manifest itself. Our survival as a species over the millennia has depended upon the ability to be mindful of what is going on around us, whether in hunting, in remaining alert for signs of danger, or in listening to the vital teachings of elders, each word of which had to be retained in the memory in the days before writing.

Mindfulness is a natural and an enjoyable skill. It only needs the space in which to flourish. We surround children with so many distractions in our modern, artificial world, that it is we who come between them and their natural abilities to stay focused upon real life. The above exercises help us to go some way towards repairing the damage.

Chapter 4

Meditation for Concentration

THE IMPORTANCE OF SIMPLICITY

When meditating with children, particularly with young children, it is essential to keep things as simple as possible. If children want more information, they will ask, and appropriate answers can be given. Again, these answers should be simple, and should not normally involve extended explanations. The benefits of meditation become apparent to children through practice rather than through words. Initially, the benefits of meditation can be summarized for the children as follows:

- helping concentration and the ability to learn
- experiencing physical relaxation
- developing imagination
- helping creativity
- finding a peaceful place within the mind that can be restful and that can help us understand and accept ourselves.

CONCLUDING THE SESSIONS

Always allow a period at the end of each meditation session in which difficulties can be aired and discussed. These difficulties typically take one of two forms. The intrusion of thoughts is the main problem facing the meditator at any level. Reassure the group that with practice thoughts become less attention-seeking. Repeat your opening advice that they should not attend to the thoughts or allow them to set off a chain of associations. Stress that they should not try too hard to push thoughts away. The harder we push, the more likely are thoughts to try to push back. It can be helpful to suggest that they see intrusive thoughts as clouds temporarily passing across the sky.

External distractions are another common problem faced by the meditator. Things such as physical discomfort, sounds in the street or elsewhere in the building, or distracting emotions can cause the attention to wander. As with thoughts, these should simply be allowed to float in and out of awareness. Counsel the group not to identify with emotions, however strong they may be. Meditation helps build equanimity, so that we are no longer at the mercy of upsetting feelings. All too often when negative emotions emerge we become those emotions (*I* am sad, *I* am afraid, *I* am angry, and so on). One of the functions of meditation is to allow us that little bit of distance between ourselves and the emotions that can threaten to engulf us.

Janis

Janis was typical of a group of adolescent girls who protested that their minds were too busy to meditate. 'I must be the world's worst,' she insisted. 'My mind won't keep still for ten seconds. I think meditation is a waste of time.' Instead of following any of the usual meditation exercises, she was recommended to keep asking herself the question, 'Why won't my mind keep still?' To her own surprise, she quickly came up with an answer that convinced her: 'I think it's because I'm afraid. I don't like being on my own physically. I always like lots of things going on around me. My mind is like the rest of me. It gets sort of lonely and anxious unless it's always busy.' This discovery proved a great help to Janis. Not only did she begin to take her meditation more seriously, she also found it helped her to enjoy her own company more and, as she put it, to 'make better friends with myself'.

Bearing the above in mind, we can now turn to meditation practices for specific areas of development, starting at the point at which we left off in the last chapter, namely concentration.

THE VALUE OF CONCENTRATION

Concentration is a prerequisite for efficient and effective learning. It represents the ability of the mind to remain focused upon what it is actually doing, without becoming distracted by other things, or by the welter of ideas, memories, daydreams and expectations that clamour for attention and all too often come between us and the task in hand. Concentration ensures that the mind is fully aware of what it is doing. Most of us have had the experience of reading a page of information, then finding we can't remember a single word of it. The mind has, in a sense, been on automatic pilot. We have read the words accurately enough, and if we had been reading aloud, other people would have been able to vouch for this. Yet nothing was transferred from that part of the mind engaged in word recognition to that part responsible for understanding and remembering what the words were intended to convey.

The workings of the automatic pilot are particularly apparent, for example, when we are driving and carry out highly skilled manoeuvres without focusing upon them at all. We drive safely from A to B but without remembering any of the details of the route. We accelerate, change gear, note the presence of other traffic, stop at traffic lights, overtake or allow ourselves to be overtaken, without thinking about it. Only when we are in dense traffic or trying to find our way through unfamiliar roads are we really likely to concentrate upon the act of driving rather than upon the ceaseless train of thoughts running through our heads.

In a way, the automatic pilot is of great use to us. There is no need to concentrate upon each of the acts of driving if we are sufficiently skilled and experienced to allow the automatic pilot to take over. Even when we are playing a musical instrument, or when we are typing as I am now, we don't have to think carefully about what we are doing with our fingers. If we did, it would probably detract from our performance, as our minds need to be focused upon the interpretation of the music, or upon the thought to which we are giving expression in our typing.

However, we have to accept that we are learning very little from the activities for which the automatic pilot is responsible. If we read a page of print on automatic pilot, with our thoughts miles away on something else, we may get each of the words correct, give them the right emphasis, pause at the commas and full stops, breathe in the right places, yet end up very little, if any, the wiser as to the sense of any of it.

The switch from automatic pilot to actual concentration comes relatively easily to most of us if the things we are doing are of personal interest. Whether we are reading, or working with our hands, or drawing or painting or whatever, we can keep our attention from straying from the task, provided it is one we actively enjoy doing. Most of us will have noticed the total concentration which a small child gives to an activity, however simple, if it captures the attention. The child is completely absorbed in what he or she is doing, and is largely oblivious to any external or internal distractors. But as the child grows older, the demands of the outside world become increasingly insistent, and he or she is faced with a daunting array of learning tasks.

Everywhere the child turns there are things that others demand must be learned, must be done, or must be avoided. By the time he or she starts school, the child is engaged upon a treadmill of activities, many of which he or she would not have voluntarily chosen, and many of which fail to engage immediate interest. Boredom begins to set in, and the mind starts to recoil from the activity upon which it is engaged in order to find more interesting things with which to occupy itself, whether these are in the outside world or in the inner world of daydreams and fantasies.

Much of the learning that is done in schools and elsewhere is highly inefficient. This is not a criticism of teachers or even of the school system. It is simply a recognition of the fact that children typically take in only a small part of the material that is presented to them. At all ages and at all levels of ability, the mind finds itself less than enthused by much of what is being asked of it, and seeks refuge in something more inspiring.

This is where mind training comes in. In the East, as mentioned earlier, the mind is spoken of as a runaway horse that must be caught and tamed and put to effective use. Left to itself, it will dissipate its energies in poorly directed and ultimately fruitless pursuits. With the proper training, however, the mind can become an awesomely effective tool, capable of taking in vast tracts of information, of exercising creativity, originality and intuition, and of accomplishing whatever it undertakes with economy and efficiency.

This mind training essentially involves learning to concentrate, whether the task concerned is something that automatically arouses interest or not. And learning to concentrate is part and parcel of learning to meditate. Of all the various methods of mind training, none surpasses meditation in helping the mind to remain attentive to whatever it is that is actually being done. And with this ability comes an increased fluency in arousing and sustaining interest. All too often tasks are abandoned before the mind has fully engaged with them and recognized their potential, but even the most mundane things can have an intrinsic fascination if we absorb ourselves in them, and keep a sense of the freshness and novelty of each moment of experience. Concentration is thus a valuable defence against boredom. And by concentrating upon a task, we are less likely to allow the mind to pass judgement upon it and to conclude that it is dull and uninteresting. The task simply becomes something that has to be done, and we can focus upon doing it to the best of our ability.

Generally, children like the idea of improving their concentration. One of the best ways in which to introduce the subject is to point out that all great sportsmen and women have remarkable powers of concentration. Tennis, cricket, golf, motor racing and many other popular sports cannot be played at any real level of proficiency without the ability to concentrate single-mindedly for long periods of time. Martial arts such as judo, aikido and kendo, where success depends upon the ability to focus upon the opponent's slightest move, and to act before he or she does, depend as much upon concentration as upon actual skills. To a great extent the same applies to many card games, to chess, and even to dominoes. Photographers, bird watchers, television and radio presenters, high court judges, airline pilots, air traffic controllers, interpreters, train drivers – the list is virtually endless – must all for long or short periods bring intense concentration to bear upon their work.

Short stories can also be of great help in arousing and sustaining children's interest in improving their powers of concentration. One example which older children enjoy concerns a Chinese martial arts teacher (a teacher of skills such as aikido, tai chi and karate) and his pupil. Each time the master and the pupil practised together, the pupil found himself unable to get the better of his master. No matter how hard he tried, the master, with effortless ease, moved first and rendered his pupil powerless. The master repeatedly explained that an expert practitioner of the martial arts must be able to concentrate so totally and so effortlessly that he is acutely aware at all times of what is going on around him, and thus instantaneously alert to any attempt at attack, no matter from which direction it might come. One day, when the master and his pupil were walking in the woods, the master called a halt in order to cook the midday rice. When the water came to the boil, the master bent down and took the lid off the cooking pot to stir the rice. Sensing that the moment had come to demonstrate that no one can be acutely aware of attack at all times, the pupil soundlessly picked up a heavy stick and struck downwards with all his force towards the master's unprotected shoulders. But before the blow could fall, the master, without looking up or pausing in his stirring, raised the lid of the cooking pot and with perfect timing warded off the blow. The stick broke upon the iron lid, and the red-faced pupil was left holding a splintered piece of wood.

In the case of the martial arts, survival may depend upon one's powers of concentration. The master's ability to concentrate was so advanced that it took in not just the rice in the cooking pot, but the whole of his environment. The faintest sound from his pupil was enough to alert him to what was about to happen. There was no need even to look around. The master's total concentration even allowed him to pinpoint the direction from which his pupil was approaching, and the exact moment when the blow would fall.

Stories such as this help to broaden the child's view of what is possible. Concentration is not only achievable, but is highly valuable to the practicalities of normal living. Although our main concern may not be to protect ourselves against sudden attack as in the case of the practitioner of the martial arts, the ability of the trained mind to focus upon a single stimulus, or to widen the range of focus to take in whatever is happening around us without losing the sharpness of our concentration, is a priceless asset. The secret is to be attuned to direct experience, rather than to be lost in the mental chatter of our own thoughts.

Children can also be helped to see that concentration not only makes them more effective in whatever they have to do, but it also allows them to do it more quickly and more efficiently. The greater the tendency to become distracted when trying to learn or accomplish something, the longer it is likely to take, the more likely it is to be done badly, and the more likely it is to have to be done again. Concentration allows children to tackle things speedily and efficiently, and then to have more time for the other things which they enjoy.

In addition, concentration helps children avoid letting their minds become preoccupied with negative feelings of frustration and resentment. It is all too easy for them to fall into the habit of telling themselves they would much rather be engaged in their own pursuits, and to feel hostility towards the task upon which they are engaged and towards the parents and teachers who insist they keep at it until the task is finished.

CONCENTRATION UPON BREATHING

No matter how complicated meditation may appear to be, it is based on the mind's ability to stay concentrated upon a given stimulus. This stimulus can be almost anything, but the usual place at which to start is the breath. There are several reasons for this.

- The breath is always with us, therefore the mind can focus upon it at anytime. This enables us to meditate at times which would otherwise be wasted (for example, when waiting for a bus, or in a queue) or to meditate whenever the mind feels the need to become peaceful.
- The breath is essential for the sustenance of life. Without breathing we would survive only a very few minutes. Consciousness of breathing thus helps body awareness, and is an excellent starting point for many other forms of meditation (e.g. the meditation upon the emotions, which we deal with in Chapter 5).
- Consciousness of breathing also helps calm the mind. Anxiety typically leads to quick, shallow breathing. By slowing down the respiration, and by breathing deeply (i.e. from the diaphragm rather than just from the upper part of the lungs) we can calm both mind and body.

The Buddha, one of the earliest recorded meditation teachers, taught his followers to concentrate upon their breathing, and made it clear that all the benefits of meditation can be gained from this method alone. Concentration upon breathing is therefore the best place at which to start the formal teaching of meditation. Even when the children are using other methods, they should always be encouraged to start by focusing for a minute or two upon the breath, so that their minds can enter the appropriate state of calm concentration. It is a good idea to use the following breathing exercise for several meditation sessions, until the children have firmly established their ability to concentrate, before going on to other exercises.

In the following exercise, and in every other one we describe, counsel the children never to feel impatient with themselves if thoughts intrude and they lose their concentration. Explain that as soon as they become aware of having lost it, they should feel grateful to their minds for drawing the fact to their attention, and then return calmly to their point of concentration.

Meditation 2: Concentrating upon the Breath

We breathe best when the body is upright, rather than in a slumped position. Now is the time to teach the children a proper meditation posture, whether they are sitting in a chair or cross-legged on the floor. Some young children can get into the so-called lotus position, resting each foot upon the opposite thigh, with disarming ease. Encourage them to do so. This kind of suppleness will stay with them throughout life if practised now. But to be comfortable for any length of time they should be on a firm cushion which raises their bottoms three to four inches (depending upon the length of their legs) from the ground.

Emphasize to the children that their backs should be straight, and their heads upright, with the eyes looking slightly downwards. The shoulders should be pulled back, but without straining. This is one of the most natural postures for the body to adopt. To begin with, the eyes should be closed, to help cut out distractions, and the fingers clasped together lightly in the lap. Then guide their meditation as follows.

> Become aware of your breathing. Focus upon the feeling of coolness at your nose when you breathe

in, and the feeling of warmth as you breathe out. Don't let your attention follow the breath into your lungs. Pretend you're a sentry who is on guard at that point, watching carefully everything that goes in and out of the gates of the city. If thoughts try to get in the way, look upon them simply as people trying to distract you, and take no notice of them.

With children who can count, you can further help their concentration by asking them to count from 'one' on the first in-breath, repeating this on the out-breath, then 'two' on the next breath, and so on up to ten. At ten, they should go back to one, and start again. Should they lose track of their counting, they should go back to one.

Prem

Prem, who comes from Thailand, was taught by his parents to meditate from a very early age, long before moving to Britain. He is popular with his fifteen-year-old classmates, not only for his calm and cheerful nature, but for his unassuming success at sport and at academic work. When invited to talk about his meditation, he said, 'I can't imagine being without it. It would be like living in only part of myself. Meditation teaches that nothing outside can touch the real me. I take things as they come. I enjoy most things, but I don't get worked up when things go wrong. It's all part of being alive. Meditation doesn't cut me off from the world. It puts me more in touch with things, but allows me to see them for what they are, without sort of being sucked in all the time.'

THE FOUNDATION OF MEDITATION

Working with the breath is the foundation for all good meditation practice. The Buddha himself went into some detail on the use of the breath, and although it is not necessary to go into these details with young children (some of these finer points in any case do not become fully relevant until the practice of meditation is quite well advanced), they can be explained to those who are older. Knowledge of these details is, however, important for the meditation teacher.

The main points concerning breathing are known in Buddhism as the 'wonderful doors' into meditation. They are six in number, namely counting, following, stopping, observing, returning and calming.

Counting

Counting each breath is a very useful aid to the beginner for two reasons. Firstly, it helps the mind to focus upon the breathing, and secondly, the very act of counting tends to prevent distracting thoughts from arising, or from dominating the mind if they do arise.

Following

Counting can become tedious once the children gain some control over their minds, so it can eventually be discontinued and the focus of attention shifted to the breathing alone. This is known as following, because the meditator simply follows the sensation of the breath as it flows past the nostrils, cool on the in-breath, and warm on the out-breath. Following does not mean that one starts to follow the breath as it flows down to the lungs. This dissipates the point of focus, and impedes concentration. Awareness should remain always at the nostrils.

Stopping

As concentration develops through following, the third door is opened, namely stopping. Stopping refers to the stopping of the discursive thoughts that usually claim our attention. The very act of concentrating upon the breathing brings about this stopping in due course. It is not something to be striven for in and of itself. If it fails to arise, then it means that following is still not being practised correctly.

Observing

When thoughts stop, or at least subside, the meditator finds that the fourth door opens, and that he or she is able to look objectively at things; that is, to observe without the intrusion of concepts. Usually when we look at anything, the mind leaps into action with definitions, judgements and a host of associations. The result is that we never actually *observe* what is in front of us (see also Chapter 3). In meditation, anything can be observed, but the starting point is usually the body. The meditator observes all the various bodily sensations that arise into consciousness. Comfort and discomfort are simply noted, and neither is judged better than the other. They are nothing but states of existence. Feelings, sensations and emotions are observed in the same way. With small children, the meditation period is too short for any detailed or lengthy observation. However, children as young as seven are well able to observe (and usually do so with great interest) what appears to be going on within their own bodies (and minds) once they have established the processes of following and stopping.

With children who find difficulty with generalized observing, you can work systematically down from the hair on the head to the tips of the toes. The children can be asked to shift their awareness from their breathing to their eyes, then to their mouths, then to the beating of their hearts, then to their arms and fingers, then to the rise and fall of their abdomens, then to their weight on the chair, and so on downwards to the tips of their toes. The effects of observing are not easy to describe. Certainly there is an increase in body awareness, as in so many of the other exercises described in this book. But there is something more which can best be described as a merging between the child who is

observing and the part of the body that is being observed.
This is an almost mystical experience, but it also makes sense
at the rational level. Consciousness is not merely in the eyes,
in the point from which the child is looking, but also in the
part of the body which is being observed (see also
Exercise 9).

Returning

This is an even harder concept to explain, and is very
definitely part of quite advanced meditation practice (though
children can reach this stage more quickly then many adults
– don't underestimate them!). It refers to the ability of the
meditator to 'return' to the source of the mind, that is, to
look at their minds when thoughts are not capturing the
attention. As already stressed, we are not our thoughts. If we
were, we would be very impermanent creatures, for thoughts
come and go in quick succession, each one holding our
attention for only a few moments. We must be more than
these fleeting mental events. Returning helps the meditator,
whether adult or child, and whether they are able fully to
articulate the experience or not, to become aware of this fact.

Calming

Calming is an inadequate word for the sixth door of
meditation. When the meditator has established awareness
first of body and then of mind, there comes a feeling of deep
peace, born of a sense of unity and harmony within oneself.
Instead of each part of the body and mind having a separate,
fragmented existence, there is only a sense of wholeness and
completeness. The arms, the legs, the heart, the abdomen
and the mind are all integral, inter-dependent aspects of
the one being. The distinction between the meditator and the
object of meditation finally disappears, and there is only a
peaceful and joyous sense of existence.

REDISCOVERING THE NATURAL STATE

Returning and calming are somewhat advanced ideas, and only older children are likely to try to put the experience into words, yet all that is happening is that the mind and the body are rediscovering their natural state. As children are much closer to this natural state than most adults, they generally have less difficulty with this rediscovery.

The mind and body can only rediscover their natural state if we let go of the barriers that separate us from this state. These barriers are created primarily by the inability to concentrate, to pay proper attention to our own being. It is rather like having a beautiful garden or a beautiful painting, and forgetting it is there because we never find the time to go and look at it. Meditation is the act of looking at our natural state, and then realizing that the person who is looking, and the natural state at which he or she is looking, are one and the same thing.

Gail, a fourteen-year-old who at first had difficulty with the idea of rediscovering the natural state, was pleased when she thought of the analogy of a mirror. 'It's like looking at your reflection, and then realizing that the person who is looking is really the person you're looking at. If you close your eyes, the reflection closes its eyes too, but you're no longer able to see it. So meditation is like opening our eyes to ourselves.'

MEDITATION WITH A MANTRA

In addition to using breathing, some children enjoy using a mantra. A mantra is simply a word or a short phrase which forms the focus of meditation. For children whose minds are particularly busy, a mantra can be the quickest way of allowing thoughts to settle down. The mantra can be anything that appeals to the child. If the meditation is being taught in a Christian or other religious context, then the mantra can be something related to God, such as 'I am a child of God'. If the context is secular, the mantra might be 'I am peaceful', 'I can be happy' or 'I believe in myself'. Alternatively one of the positive affirmations discussed below can be used. The important thing is that the children find mantras which feel right to them. They may want to discuss them with each other, or they may prefer to keep them private. Essentially it is up to them.

There are various techniques for using a mantra, but the simplest and one of the best is to repeat it only on the out-breath, and on the in-breath to look metaphorically at the empty 'space' left by the mantra. In the beginning it is best to repeat the mantra softly aloud, as this helps to establish it in the mind, but this is not possible if you are working with a group. Encourage the children to repeat the mantra softly to themselves when they are on their own, however. Emphasize that when using the mantra, the children should be still aware of their breathing, though now the focus of concentration changes from the sensation of the air at the nostrils to the awareness of sound as the breath is gently exhaled.

According to some of the great spiritual traditions, when mantra meditation is fully established, the mantra goes on repeating itself below the level of awareness (i.e. in the unconscious), even when one is not thinking about it. Its effect is thus doubly powerful.

POSITIVE THINKING

Mantras can be used in conjunction with positive affirmations, short phrases which convey positive messages to oneself. This is a particularly effective form of positive thinking.

One of the habits we acquire in childhood is to condition the mind with negative thoughts. As a result of criticism by others, of poor marks, of unkind or unthinking remarks of friends, and of unflattering comparisons with others, children get into the habit of telling themselves that they can't do things, they're not as clever/as good-looking/as popular as others, they're failures at this or that, they'll never be able to learn/understand/master something, they have no talent, they can't be trusted, and so on. Each time such thoughts occur, they tend actively to inhibit future performance. If we keep telling ourselves we can't do something, the mind and body obligingly get the message, and make sure we fail at it. We call this a self-fulfilling prophecy. The more pessimistic we are about our abilities, the more our pessimism is justified by events.

Children should always be helped to think positively about themselves – about their abilities, their appearance, their personalities. One of the best ways to repair the unwelcome conditioning that goes on is to teach children to repeat positive affirmations to themselves. Essentially, these take the form of 'I can' rather than 'I can't'. These affirmations can be very valuable in 're-programming' the mind and body, and thus in generating self-confidence in place of self-criticism and self-rejection.

Obviously these affirmations should be realistic ones. It is no good children telling themselves they can run faster than anyone else in the class when their size or build is clearly against them. Such misplaced affirmations only lead to disappointment and disillusionment, both with positive affirmations and with oneself. Affirmations should be tailored to what is realistically possible, rather than to what is clearly unattainable.

In addition to being realistic, affirmations should be as specific as possible. General statements such as 'I will succeed' are of little value. Saying 'I can learn my tables/my vocabulary list/the historical details' is much more useful. The point is to create the right mental context in which the actual learning can take place, rather than to hope the affirmation will do the learning for one.

In connection with activities such as sport, where the mind and body already know exactly what is required of them, the affirmation can be a little more general, for example 'I will play well', 'I can hit the ball cleanly' or 'I can run my fastest'. Older children can be encouraged to supplement the affirmation by actually imagining themselves playing well, hitting the ball cleanly and so on. In the area of personality, positive affirmations can include such things as 'I will be more confident when I talk to people', 'I am pleased with how I look', 'I will stay calmer when things annoy me', 'I won't worry so much about . . .' and 'If I'm myself, people will accept me'.

In all cases, children must be helped to find the appropriate words for themselves, rather than to use someone else's. Positive affirmations should feel right for the individual concerned. They should feel personal and should be used regularly, particularly when the mind is relaxed and focused as in meditation. The children should not feel they have to make a big effort of will each time they repeat the affirmation. The mind should be open, calm and accepting, and the affirmation should stand on its own, without being allowed to set off a train of associations, or to start a mental dialogue of any kind, which might invite the mind to find reasons why the affirmation should *not* be successful.

Bearing all this in mind, positive affirmations can be built into the children's meditation programme. As with a mantra, the affirmation should be repeated on each out-breath, audibly if feasible for the first few breaths, then more and more softly until it becomes silent. The mind should be aware of each word and its meaning, and the temptation to allow it to become a ritualistic mumble should be resisted if it is to remain effective.

Chapter 5

Meditation and the Emotions

DESCRIBING EMOTIONS

As a result of their work with meditation, children can become increasingly in tune with their emotional lives, and better able to recognize and talk about their feelings. We make reference to this frequently throughout the book, but emotions nevertheless warrant a chapter to themselves, as there are a number of exercises specifically designed to assist emotional self-understanding. These exercises are directed towards helping the children handle troublesome emotions – the encouragement of positive emotions such as compassion and empathy are dealt with in Chapter 11.

One of the reasons why children feel helpless in the face of strong emotions like fear and anger is that they lack any real understanding of them. Such emotions can seem to be powerful things that rise unbidden, and overwhelm them with energies they are unable to control. Part of the problem children often face in learning how to handle their own fear and anger is that they are taught by disapproving adults to see such emotions as dark forces which prompt the withdrawal of love and approval. In consequence children often distance themselves from their own emotions, thus becoming strangers to part of their own nature. It is just as bad if children are brought up in an environment which refuses to allow them to express their love and their compassion, or their sadness and their need for comfort and understanding. The more that children are allowed to acknowledge and accept their emotions, and to recognize that emotions are a natural and potentially healthy part of all our natures, the more they can learn how to express them in personally and socially appropriate and helpful ways.

The next three exercises involve helping children to experience their emotions imaginatively, and to learn how to look at them in a way which will help them to understand and handle their feelings better.

Exercise 6: Handling Fear

Start by asking the group to close their eyes and focus upon their breathing, in the usual way at the start of meditation, before continuing as follows.

> I want you to imagine you are watching a science fiction programme on television. It is a programme meant for children, but you are finding it rather scary. The hero and the heroine are fleeing along a very dark passageway deep down in the earth, and are being chased by some very frightening people down there who want to destroy them. They run along the passage, and then down a long flight of steps, with their pursuers close behind them. At the bottom of the steps the passage divides in two. They hesitate for a moment, terrified of what is behind them, but not knowing which passageway to take. In desperation they decide to turn right, but round a bend in the passage they suddenly come upon a blank wall which bars their progress. With a shout of triumph their pursuers close in upon them . . .

You can substitute any piece of imaginative story-telling for the above, but the golden rule is that it shouldn't be too frightening, and shouldn't put the children in realistic situations that would be potentially dangerous for them (i.e. avoid such things as 'you are walking home on your own on a dark night . . .'). If you have the use of a video, you can even show them a clip from a television programme, but make sure it is a programme intended for their age group, and the kind of thing they would be allowed to watch at home.

Stop the story or the film once it has begun to generate mild amounts of fear, and ask the children, with their eyes closed, to explore the feeling of fear within their bodies. Where is this fear? How do they recognize it as fear? How exactly does it feel? Why is it unpleasant? Then ask them to relax, and allow the feeling of fear to drain away, leaving them calm and happy.

Help your children to realize that the more they know about fear, the less reason they have to be afraid of it! Fear is only the various feelings within the body which they have just identified. When they relax, the feelings of fear just fade away. Allow them the opportunity to talk about the feelings they have just experienced.

Then discuss with them the value of fear. Boys in particular have to get away from the idea that there is anything 'unmanly' about being afraid. Explain to the children how fear can help to warn us of danger, and can give us a sudden burst of energy to help us run away if we have to. Fear thus helps us to protect ourselves. It also teaches us that we are right to be wary of the unknown, and of lonely and dark places. Therefore there is nothing to be ashamed of in fear; it is natural and potentially helpful.

However, we need to be able to handle our fear, to keep it within proportion, and to recognize when there is a real need for it, and when it just arises through habit or through our mistaken ideas as to what is really threatening and what is not. In essence, what you are doing is helping the children to make friends with their fear, so that they can see it as a very useful servant, rather than as a dreaded master.

One group of eight-year-olds asked if they could make a list of all the things of which they were afraid, and then used the more common ones as themes for meditation. The result was a growing pride in their ability to look calmly at imaginary fears instead of trying to run away from them.

Exercise 7: Dealing with Anger

A similar exercise to that used for fear can be used to explore anger. You can tell the children a story that is likely to make them feel some anger – anything to do with unfairness to children, abuse of the environment or cruelty to animals usually does the trick. Or again, you can show them a clip from a children's television programme which is likely to make them feel angry on behalf of the child or children whose story they are watching. Once again, ask them to identify where the anger is in their bodies, and how it feels and how they recognize it as anger. Then ask them to relax and feel the anger, like the fear, draining away.

In the discussion that follows, encourage them to describe the sort of situations that make them angry. Then prompt them to see that anger, like fear, has a very useful function. It helps us to protect ourselves when attacked, and to stand up for others who are being treated unfairly or who cannot stand up for themselves. But like fear, anger should be a servant and not a master. The more children can understand their anger, and the kind of situations which make them angry, the more they are able to see where anger is justified, and where they should just relax and let it slip away.

Exercise 8: Dealing with Sadness

Sadness is another often troublesome emotion that can be dealt with in a similar way to fear and anger. Once more, the stimulus can be a story or a video clip that, without arousing emotions that are too overwhelming, allows the children to feel sad or sympathetic or concerned for another child, an animal, a broken toy, a lost doll, or whatever seems to be appropriate.

Ask the children once more, with their eyes closed, to locate the sadness in themselves, and to explore where it is located, how it actually feels, and how they know that it is sadness. Then ask them to relax and feel the sadness slipping away, to be replaced with peace and a sense of happiness.

Discuss with the children other times in their lives when they have felt sad, and listen to the various reasons for their sadness. Ask them the purpose of sadness – why do we have the potential inside ourselves for this particular emotion? If possible, the discussion should bring out the point that sadness is linked to sympathy and concern for others and for ourselves, and can prompt us to do something to help those who are suffering. Help them to see that sadness is thus a very valuable emotion, and only becomes a problem if it is there for no reason or if it goes on too long. Make sure the children understand that through understanding more about this emotion, and through meditation and relaxation, they can learn how to handle their sadness more effectively.

TO SUM UP ABOUT EMOTIONS

Essentially what the children are learning to do in these exercises is to observe their own feelings without identifying too closely with them and becoming overwhelmed by them. You are not trying to stop children from feeling emotions (which would be to blunt their sensitivity and interfere with their humanity), or to repress and bottle up their emotions (which would store up trouble for them later in life, for repressed emotions are one of the major causes of adult neurosis). You are not trying to prevent them from expressing their emotions, as the expression of emotions is often a necessary safety valve. To sum up and re-emphasize what we have already said, you are trying to help them to:

- recognize and accept the presence of their emotions
- stop feeling guilty or weak when experiencing emotions, and to understand that emotions are a natural aspect of human life
- get to know and understand the exact nature of their emotions, at both the psychological and the physical levels, and to understand the purpose of emotions

- reach a better appreciation of when emotions are appropriate and when they arise merely through habit or through misunderstanding
- recognize that it is possible to let go of emotions instead of allowing them to become too overwhelming.

Children vary greatly in their sensitivity, and your concern must always first and foremost be to protect this sensitivity. It is also important to realize that those children who experience emotions *less* deeply than others should not be made to think that they are in any way inferior as a result. Some may not feel even the smallest stirring of fear in response to the story you tell them or the video clip you show them in Exercise 6. Some may not feel anger or sadness in response to the material in the other two exercises. That's fine. They must be who they are. You don't want them to feel inferior or superior to others as a result. Neither do you want them to pretend to experience emotions that they are not actually experiencing.

Such children will nevertheless still gain benefit from the exercises which will help prepare them for those bigger occasions when they actually do experience the emotions concerned. Rest assured that time spent in work of this kind is never wasted, even if children are unable to see the value of it until some time later.

Chapter 6

Meditation for Relaxation

PHYSICAL TENSION

Relaxation was the first of the benefits from meditation we listed in Chapter 1. Physical tension creeps up upon children unnoticed, leading to the slump in posture, the hunched shoulders and the drooping neck that are often all too evident by late adolescence. Physical tension is the cause of most of the muscular aches and pains we learn to live with as we grow older, the twinges we tend to feel from early adulthood onwards when we move suddenly, the stiffness and even the physical tiredness we experience at the end of the day.

It needn't be like this. Children are not born tense. Watch small children as they curl up with their toys on the floor, when they run and when they play. The idea of pulled muscles, creaking joints and strained ligaments is alien to small children. Their bodies serve them much as nature intended.

There is a range of reasons why physical tensions start in childhood. One of the most important is that children (like adults) spend much of their time with muscles tensed for physical activity, but with insufficient opportunity to engage in this activity. Nature designed human beings for an active physical life, and our bodies are not yet adapted to the fact that in our gadgety, automated, television and car orientated world, many of the things we do require very little in the way of muscular effort. As a result, from childhood onwards there is a tendency to take too little physical exercise, and for energy to remain as undischarged tension in nerves and muscles. As an analogy, think of twisting up an elastic band, and then only half releasing it.

Another reason why children build up tension from an early age is that they frequently suffer inner conflict. Many of their activities are undertaken at the request or command of adults. When these requests or commands are unwelcome, an inner struggle goes on between the need to obey their elders, and the desire to resist and please themselves. The result is that one set of impulses moves the child forward, and another tries to hold him or her back. An appropriate analogy this time could be a piece of rope with its ends pulled simultaneously in opposite directions.

A third reason for tension is that early on in life children brace themselves physically against criticism, much as they would if they were about to receive a physical blow. In the long evolutionary history of the human race, threats to safety have usually come in the form of physical attack, leading to an instinctive tensing of every muscle in order to defend ourselves or to run away (the so-called fight or flight response). Verbal attack has been a feature of our lives only since men and women developed the ability to talk (a comparatively recent development in the history of evolution), and the body hasn't yet had time to evolve an appropriate response to this kind of threat. Thus from an early age we will respond as if the threat were physical, and pump adrenalin and nor-adrenalin into the bloodstream, raise the heart rate and the blood pressure, and brace every muscle in the body.

A further cause of tension in children is the repression of emotion. Children are all too often punished for showing powerful emotions such as fear or anger, and even given the impression that there is something naughty or wicked about these natural impulses. Very often (particularly in the case of co-operative and obedient children), the result is that they quickly learn to 'hold on' to their emotions instead of expressing them. This 'holding on' involves yet again high levels of physical tension. Frequently these tensions become habitual, building themselves into children's posture and into the way they live their lives. When working with adults, some massage and bodywork therapists claim that by locating and releasing areas of physical tension within the body, they can help clients recall long-forgotten memories of traumatic childhood incidents, and go on to release the long-repressed emotions associated with them.

This is not an argument in favour of always allowing children to express their emotions, no matter how destructive. We live in a social world, and children must learn to think not only of themselves but of the impact of their behaviour upon others. Furthermore, extreme expressions of rage or dislike can bring their own tensions. However, it is an argument for helping children to acknowledge and discuss their emotions, and for helping them to find acceptable ways of releasing the energies concerned. It is also an argument for teaching children relaxation techniques which can help them remain naturally calmer in the face of stress . . . and one of the very best of these techniques is meditation.

The word 'relaxation' is insufficient on its own to describe the desirable habits of body management that arise from meditation, such as the ability to let go of tension, and the ability to become more aware of the body, so that the moment tension arises it can be identified and released. The following meditation will help the children to release physical tension, while body awareness is covered in greater depth in Chapter 7.

One way of helping children let go of physical tension is to play some soothing music, and encourage them to flop down on the bed or on the floor and progressively relax each group of muscles, starting from the feet and working up to the eyes and the muscles of the scalp. Unfortunately they can't spend all their time listening to soothing music and flopping down on the floor. Once they are back on their feet, the tensions are all too likely to re-occur. They therefore need to be able to stay relaxed when their bodies are active once more, and as they go about the business of the day. Children need good body tone and posture, and at the same time an awareness of how they can maintain this for themselves. Exercises involving releasing tension are usually easy for young children to carry out. Often adults experience much more difficulty – sufficient evidence, if we need it, of the value of maintaining or developing the right attitude towards our bodies early in life, that is, an attitude of appreciation and respect which prevents us from putting the body under unnecessary stress or neglecting its care and requirements. Adolescents can have particular difficulty with this at times.

Jerry

Jerry, in his final year at school, revealed his tension by talking in quick, jerky, breathless phrases. He was encouraged to meditate upon his breathing, and to repeat the sound 'so-ha' softly to himself (or under his breath when sitting with classmates) on each out-breath. After practising this for several sessions, he was invited to try to keep this relaxed experience in mind when talking to others.

Jerry noticed a big improvement almost immediately – and so did his friends. He also noticed that his thinking became more measured and more effective. Instead of his thoughts tumbling over themselves as his speech had done, they seemed, as he put it, to begin to flow gently and creatively.

Meditation 3: Letting Go of Physical Tension

Encourage the children to sit with spines straight, heads upright (but not pulled unnecessarily back on the neck), both feet flat on the floor, and hands clasped lightly in the lap. This relaxed posture is not only good for the body, but it also helps the mind to remain lightly alert rather than drifting.

When the meditation is over, the children should be asked to open their eyes gently, and then to stand up while retaining the feeling of relaxed alertness that they have just been experiencing. If circumstances permit, ask them to move silently around the room, picking up and putting down objects, lacing or unlacing shoes, in fact doing any of the physical activities in which they engage during the day, but all the time maintaining their peaceful fame of mind and relaxed body.

Chapter 7

Meditation for Body Awareness

THE IMPORTANCE OF BODY AWARENESS

We carry our bodies around with us from the cradle to the grave. For much of the time, we are unaware of them unless they are giving us trouble. This is reasonable enough; the mind should be free to concentrate upon other things. However, this lack of body awareness means that the tensions discussed in the previous chapter can all too often creep up on us unawares. Children and adults alike may get out of bed in the morning in a rested and relaxed state, but by the evening be like coiled watchsprings, irritable and irritating, yet without any real awareness of when and how relaxation gave way to non-relaxation.

Tensions can even develop during pleasurable activities. If you are a car driver, demonstrate this to yourself by trying a simple little experiment. Without relaxing your attention on the road ahead, check your shoulder, neck and back muscles from time to time. The likelihood is that you will find them tense. Relax them, then try again a little later. Once more, you are likely to find they have tensed up. None of this tension is necessary in order to drive the car. Now check which muscles really do need to be involved. Unless you are engaged in a difficult manoeuvre, often it is only those of the hands, the lower arms and the feet.

Try the same exercise when sitting at your desk, or when engaged in some domestic chore, even when talking to others – particularly if they are people you don't know well or with whom you feel rather uneasy. Notice the tension. If it isn't in the shoulders and the neck, check the eye muscles, the muscles of the forehead and scalp, the hands, the stomach and the knees. Again, in many cases you will find that unnecessary strain has unconsciously been allowed to build up.

Body awareness prevents this strain from happening, and the best time to learn body awareness is in childhood. A good exercise to use with children is to ask them to sweep their awareness through their bodies starting with the feet. This technique is detailed in the following exercise. Young children also like to play games which involve moving the awareness around the body in response to instructions from a partner.

Exercise 9: Experiencing Body Awareness

Ask the children to shut their eyes, then touch each child lightly on the backs of the hands, the face and the arms with a variety of different objects (a feather, the bristles of a toothbrush, a piece of apple, a leaf or flower, a glass bottle, a piece of material and so on). Then ask them to identify the object which is doing the touching, and the area that is being touched. Ask them to be aware of the different sensations involved. If these sensations can be named, so much the better, but this is not essential – the purpose of the exercise is to increase body awareness rather than to test vocabulary.

Next ask the children to put their awareness in different parts of the body as called out by you. ('Be aware of your left knee, now the middle finger of your right hand, now your nose, now your mouth, now your toes . . .') If this proves difficult, the children can be asked to move the part of the body concerned each time you call it out.

Finally, ask the children to allow their awareness to move around the body, starting either with the feet and moving upwards, or with the head and moving downwards. You can extend the game by trying to 'guess' in which part of the body the child is placing his or her awareness (slight involuntary movements often give the necessary clues).

Children can be helped to feel the difference between tension and relaxation by being asked to tense the muscles at each of the points you mention, and then to let the tension go. Few of them ever have any real difficulty with this.

BODY AWARENESS AND CONSCIOUSNESS

A valuable side-effect of the last exercise is that from an early age children can be helped to see that consciousness does not live in only one part of the body. Usually when Westerners are asked where their consciousness is, they reply that it is in the head, or just behind the eyes. This is in fact pure habit. In the East, people are often more likely to point to the pit of their stomach, the solar plexus, the place where emotions are most keenly felt, and where we have the highest concentration of nerves in the body after the brain.

The truth is that consciousness is not located exclusively in any one part of our anatomy. Certainly the brain is involved in consciousness, but this doesn't mean that consciousness resides inside the brain. If we cut a finger, the consciousness of pain is felt in the finger, not inside the head. The reason we imagine we live in our heads or just behind the eyes, is that under normal circumstances visual sensations are the ones of which we are most readily aware.

Read through this paragraph, and then try for yourself the following brief experiment. Close your eyes, and ask yourself where your awareness happens to be now. Nine people out of ten will answer that it is in the sensations felt by their closed eyelids. This experiment demonstrates two things. Firstly, you don't 'live' behind your eyes – you've just proved that by moving your awareness to a place in front of your eyes, namely to your eyelids. And secondly, you've demonstrated how fixated most of us are on the sensations around our eyes. Even when our eyes are closed, our awareness lingers around the sensations closest to them, namely those felt in the eyelids.

Ask the children where they feel themselves to 'live' within their bodies. If they say in their heads or behind their eyes, ask them to try the experiment I've just described. When their consciousness has moved into their eyelids, ask them to move it further – to the tip of the nose, for example, then down to the lips, to the throat as they swallow, to the trunk as they breathe in and out, to the backs of their thighs resting against the chair on which they are sitting, to the soles of their feet touching the ground. If they have difficulty with the exercise, ask them to place their finger on the parts of the body as they are mentioned.

Exercise 10: Co-ordinated Movement

Another valuable exercise in body awareness for children is to practise co-ordinated movement. Ask them to hold their hands in front of their chests, palms facing towards each other and about six inches apart. Now tell them to move their hands further and further apart, while trying to remain aware of both hands, as if they were connected together by invisible cords. Then get them to bring the hands together once more, and take them apart again. Ask the children now to be aware of the parts of the body involved in this movement – the lower and upper arms, and the shoulders.

Now ask them to bend forward and touch the floor, putting their awareness in their fingers as they reach out towards the ground. Then repeat the exercise, but this time with the awareness in the small of the back, and with the arms, hands and fingers hanging loose, simply obeying the force of gravity.

AVOIDING PHYSICAL STRAINS

In addition to building body awareness, the previous exercise is a wonderful way of avoiding back strains later in life. All too often when we are told in childhood to touch our toes, our awareness goes straight to the sensation of reaching downwards with the fingertips, and the back (from where the movement actually comes) is ignored completely. The usual result is that the back tenses up, the last thing we want to happen as tension is the major cause of back problems later in life. If the awareness is placed in the back, however, and the arms, hands and fingers allowed simply to dangle in front of the body, the feeling is quite different. The back is much more relaxed, and the exercise becomes much easier. Try it for yourself. If you suffer from back ache, it's one of the best ways of re-educating your mind to be more aware of, and much kinder towards, the muscles and ligaments upon which our upright posture depends, and which all too often begin to give us trouble as we grow older.

KINHIN

In Zen Buddhism, there is a walking meditation called kinhin. In kinhin, the meditator practises what might be called stillness in movement. Each foot is lifted slowly and with infinite precision, and placed exactly the same distance ahead (usually about four inches), and the weight allowed to flow evenly forward. There is nothing forced or jerky or unbalanced about any aspect of the movement. The meditator is literally meditating upon each minute shift in position by the body. For him or her, the body is a complete unit rather than a set of separate, uncoordinated parts, and the mind is at one with the body, rather than distracted by its own thoughts. The moment the concentration wavers and the meditator loses this mind-body connection, the inevitable result is a stumble and a loss of physical balance.

Chrissy
Chrissy, a young teenager who had found great difficulty in keeping still during sitting meditation, took to kinhin at once. It was noticeable how balanced her body became as she moved slowly forward; there was no hesitation and no

wobbling, an indication of the depth of her concentration. After the session was over, she stayed behind to talk about her experience, explaining that her meditation had 'included all of me, as if my mind was moving physically with my body'. She was fortunate in having a long straight path in her garden at home which was ideal for kinhin, and she took to using it for her meditation, retreating to the upstairs landing on wet days. In addition to helping steady her mind, she found that kinhin made her more aware of her body throughout the day, thus improving her posture and helping her feel more confident about the way she looked.

In the following exercise, the children are performing a version of kinhin. In doing so, they are carrying their body awareness into the movements of everyday life, and helping not only to maintain a state of relaxation, but also to still and focus the mind. This exercise cannot be practised too often.

Meditation 4: Moving with Awareness

If you are working with a group of children, and have a large room in which to operate, ask them to move round as softly and gently as they can, as if they were treading on eggshells, or stalking someone through the woods and avoiding stepping on twigs. Tell them to be aware of each movement they make – the thigh muscle as they lift the back leg and move it forward, the foot as it comes to the ground, the trunk as it advances in space, their hands and arms as they help maintain balance, and so on.

SELF-AWARENESS

A development of body awareness is self-awareness. This is more subtle, and is often only suitable for older children, but the aim is to be aware not just of bodily movements, but of the strange, abstract, mysterious 'self' that lies behind them.

In the next exercise, the children are invited to carry out a task with their attention centred all the time upon a particular part of their upper body, and to be aware at the same time of the person to whom it belongs. Obviously the task you choose for them must be such that they can carry it out in perfect physical safety, but the idea of centring upon a particular part of the body will already be familiar to them from the previous exercises.

Meditation 5: Self-remembering

Choose a simple activity such as a walk around a garden or a school playing field, which can be carried out individually and in silence. Ask the children to focus upon their left arms (or their right arms if they are left-handed), and explain the activity as follows.

> This is a simple game in which you have to see if you can carry out a task while keeping your attention focused upon your left arm. The task is to walk around the playing field, remembering your left arm all the time. Be conscious of its movement as you walk, of how the muscles feel, of whether it is hot or cold, of how it relates to the rest of your body. If you forget your left arm, bring your attention gently back to it.
>
> At the same time, be aware of the person to whom the arm belongs. Be aware of the person who moves this arm, who feels the sensations within it, who can clasp or unclasp the fingers, who can use it to touch things, who can make it obey his or her wishes. Try to keep this awareness at all times.

The exercise should only take a few minutes if you decide to use it with younger children, but with those who are older it can go on for a quarter of an hour or more.

Follow-up

The exercise should be repeated on a number of occasions, varying the part of the body which the children are remembering (legs and arms are best, as they are the parts most involved in movement). You can also vary the task, so that it includes movements other than walking.

Discuss with the children any difficulties they may have had, and if they found that their self-remembering was easier when they were focusing upon one part of the body rather than another, or when engaged in one task rather than in others. If it was, they may be able to suggest a reason, thus showing an increasing readiness to explore their experience of living in and with their own bodies.

MORE ADVANCED SELF-REMEMBERING

At its deepest level, self-remembering is being aware of the fact that we are conscious, that we are always the agent in our experiences of the world. There is no need to try to explain this rather difficult concept to younger children. It is far more important for them simply to experience it, and thus to allow this level of consciousness to develop of itself, than for them to become lost in attempts to talk about it.

The next exercise works at this deeper level. It is similar to the last one in that the children are asked to engage in a simple, safe task such as walking around a garden or a school playing field, but this time their remembering is directed somewhat differently.

Meditation 6: Inclusive Self-remembering

Introduce the activity as follows.

> We're going to try a game similar to the one in which we concentrated upon a part of the body, but this time, as you walk around, I would like you to

repeat quietly to yourself, '*I* am walking', '*I* am seeing or hearing . . .' whatever it is you are seeing or hearing etc. If thoughts come into your mind, don't follow them, just tell yourself, '*I* am thinking'. If you feel an emotion of any kind, tell yourself, '*I* am feeling . . .' whatever it is you are feeling.

When the exercise is finished, the children will want to share their experiences with you. After you have listened to them, ask simply, 'Who is this "I" who was experiencing all the things you have just been talking about?' Don't press for an answer (which in any case is always difficult to put into words). The question itself will be enough to set the children wondering.

After pondering the question 'Who is this I?', one group of adolescents quickly decided it was nothing to do with their names, their relationships, their appearances or even their personalities and the things they liked and disliked. They concluded it was best described by such things as 'just being alive', 'an experience of being', 'knowing I'm here', 'happiness, sadness, whatever I'm feeling at this moment', 'just mind', and 'nothing in particular'. It was clear they had made a good start, and would continue to ponder the question.

THE NATURE OF THINGS

As we grow older, we take not only the outside world and the business of living, but also the individual who is doing this living, very much for granted. We become our own habit. We stop asking questions about ourselves, our origins, our destiny, and about the strange fact that we should exist at all. The purpose of the following exercise is to help the children not only to keep alive their wonder at themselves, but to help them (if they wish) to go deeper in their exploration of this wonder.

The next exercise continues and extends the philosophical

theme of the previous exercise and introduces the concept of things ceasing to be themselves. The exercise is a valuable adjunct to formal meditation in that once again it takes the children deeply into the nature of 'things'. Meditation helps the mind to penetrate into its own nature and into the whole experience of what it is to be alive. If we are not to remain strangers in the world, never seeing below the surface of things, we need to escape from a stereotyped, restricted way of looking at and understanding our surroundings. Children experience life with a freshness and a sense of novelty which brings with it mystery, excitement and limitless possibilities. If we can help them to retain this freshness, rather than smothering it with the notion that things are merely what they seem, and that there is only one 'correct' way of looking at the world, then they will continue to have access to the richness and originality of thinking that underlies not only creativity, but also that curiosity and excitement which is essential to a joy and delight in living.

Exercise 11: When Do Things Cease to be Themselves?

This exercise can be presented theoretically, but it gains a great deal if it takes the form of a practical demonstration. Show the class an object that can be dismantled, piece by piece. It may be a model aircraft or car, or a box or a doll's house that slots together, or something you have made specially for the purpose. Ask the children to name the object. Then begin to take it to pieces, asking them after each piece is removed whether it still continues to be the car, the house or the box that it was at the start. Many different opinions are likely to be given, but the children will gradually come to see that the car, for example, isn't the wheels, or the engine, or the seats, or the doors, or the body, or any of the individual components. So what is a 'car'? Does it really exist? Or is it simply a collection of separate objects, none of which is itself a car? By the same token, what is a table when we separate it into four legs and a top? What is a chair when we take it apart in the same way? What is a tune when we take away individual notes? What is a word when we take away individual letters? And so on.

What we are really doing with this exercise is showing that the whole is greater than the mere sums of the parts. By putting things together in a certain way, whether those things be wheels, table or chair legs, the notes of a piece of music or the letters in a word, we create something that is much more than the total we get when we add up a line of figures. But what is this 'something'? Can it really be said to 'exist'? And yet quite clearly it does. We can experience it, think about it and talk about it.

Finally, the children can apply the same exercise to themselves. Are we merely a collection of bits and pieces, arms, legs, brains, thoughts, stomachs and so on, or is there something more? If so, what is it? And when people change their moods, the way they look or the way they talk, are they the same people? Are the children the same people that they were last year, the year before that, or the years before they started school?

QUESTIONING ONESELF

There is another form of meditation which further extends exploration into the nature of things. It is suitable for older children, particularly adolescents.

It would be a mistake to introduce this self-questioning meditation before the other exercises we have detailed so far, as until the meditative practice is reasonably well established, children and adults alike can become distracted by the novelty of the technique, with the result that they not only fail to master the more basic meditative skills, but they also fail to get answers to their questions at anything other than the conscious level, and may finally come to reject the exercise as being of little use to them.

Meditation 7: Self-questioning

Explain to the children that self-questioning consists of using a question as the focus for meditation, repeating it on each breath (as with a mantra – see Chapter 4). The specific questions the children choose to ask are very much up to them. But generally, the questions should relate to their own being, rather than to external events. They may want to ask how they can help others more, or be better liked, or work harder, or find long-term goals, or where happiness lies, or (at the deepest level of all) 'Who am I?' Explain that the difference between this and the usual way in which we question ourselves is that:

- the mind is in a focused and concentrated meditative state
- a single question is used, and the mind is prevented from straying from it
- no attempt is made to answer the question consciously; in fact conscious attempts are distractions to be avoided
- the meditator waits patiently for the answer, without urgency or anxiety; of course he or she would like an answer, but if it fails to arise, no matter. The importance lies in the question itself, and in the meditator's recognition that it is worth asking.

Explain that if an answer arises, they should note it, but not explore it. They should either go on asking the question, or return to the breathing or whatever focus of meditation you have asked them to use. It is only after the meditation is over that the answer should be taken up by the conscious mind, and examined for relevance. Also, tell them that if answers come they shouldn't be accepted slavishly. They are simply food for thought.

Children often feel the need for direction and guidance, and self-questioning during meditation helps them realize they have a wise friend inside them who is always there and always ready to help. But the inner friend, like friends in the outside world, is not infallible. His or her answers must always be scrutinized by the conscious mind, which can then accept or reject them as the case may be.

It is interesting to speculate on where the answers that arise in meditations of this kind come from. Do they originate in creative, insightful levels of the meditator's unconscious, or do they come from some source outside the mind? The answer depends largely upon one's own belief system, and it is best to leave it at that.

Chapter 8

Meditation for Creativity

THE CREATIVE POWER OF THE MIND

The creative power of the mind is virtually limitless. At a physiological level, we only use a small percentage of the brain's capacity for thinking and problem-solving, while at a psychological level, with the right stimulation and guidance, we are capable of original and effective productions in most branches of the arts and sciences. The mind is a well of untapped potential.

Much of our creative ability is stifled in the early years by the conscious mind. Creative impulses arise from the unconscious (we are still unsure of the exact mechanisms involved), and are then submitted to scrutiny by the conscious mind. But all too often the conscious mind becomes over-critical. Children are taught by others that they are 'no good' at drawing or at music or at painting or writing poetry, and their creative impulses are discouraged and devalued. In this way, inhibitions increasingly come between them and their creativity. Barriers are erected between the conscious and the unconscious levels of the mind, and children are literally educated out of their creative abilities.

Psychologically this is intensely damaging. Children are born with a fundamental drive to create. Through creativity, inner energies that long for expression throughout life are satisfied, energies which have been behind not only humanity's achievements in the arts and in the sciences, but behind the practical business of utilizing natural resources in order to survive. Without creativity, the human race would not have made it through the long centuries of evolution up to the present day.

Any such energy which is not channelled into socially acceptable forms and given full expression is likely to cause psychological problems. The mind feels restless and unfulfilled, searching for something without knowing quite what it is. There is a feeling that some undefined potential is going to waste, and that something precious is being denied the light of day.

In addition to its innate energy, creativity has a further function in that it allows emotions and feelings to be expressed in satisfying and healthy ways. Singing, dancing, painting, writing and sculpting have from the beginnings of recorded history served as channels for humanity's deepest hopes, fears and insights. They serve as outward revelations of our inner states of mind, help us communicate with each other, and draw men and women together into shared expression of feelings. Creativity, in a real sense, serves as the voice of the community, articulating harmonies and tensions, and helping to make us comprehensible to each other.

All young children love to create. Two of the first actions of the very young are to sing and to scribble. Throughout the primary school years, art remains the activity most children best enjoy, followed by physical movement. Only later, as they grow older and become examination-orientated, and convinced either that there is no 'future' in artistic ability or that they lack the necessary skills, do they turn away from these 'non-serious' subjects and deny an integral part of their birthright.

Creativity is the ability to go beyond the known and the customary, and to find new ways of doing things. Without creativity, the human race would go on doing things in the same way, generation after generation, and would have failed to evolve beyond instinctive, animalistic behaviour.

Psychologists recognize that creativity, whether in the arts or in the sciences, expresses itself in terms of three things – *fluency* (the ability to generate a range of ideas), *flexibility* (the ability to draw these ideas from many different sources) and *originality* (the ability to come up with new ideas). For example, a simple creativity test asks children to think of as many uses as they can for a house brick. A response that is merely fluent would involve numerous ideas, but all drawn from the same category (e.g. the use of a brick as a load-bearing object). On the other hand, a response that is both fluent and flexible would recognize that in addition to being load-bearing, a brick can weigh things down, can be used as a missile, as a means of storing heat, as an obstacle, as a metaphor and so on. A response that is fluent, flexible and original would also contain some unusual uses, such as grinding the brick into powder, and using the powder for cleaning and polishing.

Many leading artists and scientists have testified to the fact that their most creative ideas have come to them in moments when their minds were relaxed, or when they were daydreaming, or even sleeping. Of course, they would have prepared the ground by study and experiment beforehand, but it seems that the unconscious, which is the source of creative ideas, can often best bring material up into the conscious mind when the latter is in a quiescent mood.

Meditation is one of the most effective ways of achieving this mood, and when children meditate, creative ideas often arise unbidden. It seems likely that meditation also helps creativity at other times, keeping open the channels between the unconscious and the conscious mind, thus allowing creative ideas to emerge into awareness. Insight and intuition, as valuable in the sciences as they are in the arts, make their presence felt, and the mind becomes increasingly free to enjoy more of its own richness.

There are many meditations that actively encourage creativity, partly through helping with visualization (see also Meditation 11), and partly through heightening the meditator's inner awareness. The following three exercises are a good starting point for developing creativity. The first introduces and encourages creativity, while the two that follow deal more specifically with fluency, flexibility and originality.

Meditation 8: Encouraging Creativity

After establishing meditative awareness as usual, ask the children to visualize the following scene.

> Imagine there is a white screen just between and above your closed eyes. See the outline of a house appear on the white screen, just a plain outline, without any details. Now see the front door appear. Now see each of the windows. Now the chimneys. And now the house is being coloured. Next, you can see the details of the garden, perhaps with trees and flowers and a pond. Then the birds arrive, and the squirrels come to look for food on the lawn. Now the sun begins to shine, and fills the garden with light and shadows, and the front door opens and children come out into the garden to play.

The advantage of using this as a meditation instead of asking the children to draw each of these things is that their visual imagination is likely to be much better developed than their skills with a pencil or a paintbrush. Making the link between what is seen in the imagination and what is reproduced on paper can come later during an art lesson (and especially in connection with the work arising from Exercise 5). The more vividly a child is able to visualize a scene, the more chance he or she has to capture its essence on paper. But in any event, skill in drawing is not the object of the exercise. Creativity in a drawing is apparent in the details it includes, and in the arrangement of the details, rather than in the quality of draughtmanship.

This meditation can take almost any subject as its starting point. Once the children have worked with the picture of a house, they can meditate upon a scene at the seaside or in the mountains or on a farm, or be asked to visualize a sporting scene, or a children's party, or an episode from an exciting film, or a zoo full of animals, or even a busy street. As the work progresses, include scenes that on the face of it have little to offer visually. The more inventive children become, the more able they are to see the possibilities in the most unpromising material. For example, they can be asked to work with a foggy afternoon, or with a pond in winter, or with a quiet country lane. Don't ask the children to 'draw' or to 'put in' details. Instead, tell them to 'see' these details appear. They should not be making a conscious effort to 'create' something. As in a dream, the unconscious will create things by itself if left to get on with it. Children, with their spontaneous approach, are far better at this than are adults. When faced with the same exercise, some adults find themselves staring at nothing but the blank screen. The only advice to give to them is patience. Details will emerge eventually. The problem seems to be that the conscious mind, taken aback by the invitation to allow things to emerge by themselves, regards the task as impossible, and therefore actually inhibits the creative images from appearing.

Fiona

Fiona, an eleven-year-old with a rather unsettled home background, found the above exercise not only helped her to work more creatively in school, it also enabled her to calm some of her worries and to go to sleep more easily at night. Her favourite starting point was a woodland just behind her home. 'I see it with all the leaves just coming on the trees in spring, so that I can see the sky through the branches. I look around to see if there are any flowers, and sometimes I find bluebells and celandines and wild primroses. Then sometimes a rabbit or a bird comes to say hello. Once I heard the voices of my friends, and sometimes when I fall asleep I dream I'm still in the wood, and it makes me happy.'

Meditation 9: Fluency and Flexibility

A rather different approach to creativity is encouraged by the following meditation that invites the children to generate as many different versions of the same object as possible. Ask the children to visualize a blank screen as before, then continue as follows.

> Allow a cat to appear on your screen. Look closely at the cat. Notice its colour, the length of its tail, and the way it is sitting or standing. Now look at its face, and see that it has a very contented expression, as if it has just been given some cream. Now see the expression change to a watchful one, as if it suspects there is a mouse under the chair. Now see it change to a disappointed expression, as it realizes there is no mouse there after all. Now the expression changes to a happy one, as the cat thinks she hears the children coming home from school. Now it changes to a cross expression, as she realizes the children are going off to play without first coming into the house. Now the expression becomes sleepy, and now hungry . . .

You can carry on with as many variations as you like. The children are experiencing their ability to change what they are seeing in a variety of quite subtle ways.

You can use other subjects in addition to the cat, for example:

- a country scene in which the seasons change through spring, summer, autumn and winter
- a day that goes from sunny to cloudy, and then to stormy and back again
- an artist's sketch pad on which the artist quickly draws the same scene from different viewpoints
- the children themselves looking in a mirror and seeing their reflections in a variety of different clothes – school clothes, best clothes, summer clothes, winter clothes, pyjamas, sports clothes.

Don't linger too long over any one scene. The purpose of the meditation is to experience fluency and flexibility, and the ingenuity with which the mind can generate creative scenes.

Meditation 10: Originality Exercise

The last two meditation exercises encourage originality, but there are even more specific ways of doing so, as in the following exercise. Again, start by asking the children to visualize a blank screen.

> On the screen, you can see an inventor standing in his (or her) workroom. The inventor is going to invent a new way of travelling. He has had enough of cars and ships and bicycles and aeroplanes, and is going to invent something that no one else has ever thought of. Look at how he gathers together all the bits and pieces that are going to be needed. Now see how these are put together. Notice how the finished object looks. Where is it intended to travel? Look to see whether it really is something new or not. Look to see if you think it is going to work, and if you would like to ride in it.

Instead of something in which to travel, the inventor could be working on a new writing machine perhaps, or a new way of digging the garden or washing the dishes or making the beds or cleaning the car. Choose something linked to the children's own experience, and therefore likely to hold their interest.

When discussing the results of this exercise, take care not to praise some children's originality over that of others. Each time a child thinks of something that is new *for him or her*, originality has been demonstrated, even if many thousands of people have thought up the very same thing in the past. Originality can be all too easily stifled if children are led to believe that anything they come up with has already been thought of before, and that their originality is of no value compared to that of the great men and women of the past or even to that of other children. Reflect on how many adults are held back in their creative thinking by just such misguided notions!

Chapter 9

Meditation for Imagination

THE IMPORTANCE OF IMAGINATION

Certain meditation exercises are of enormous benefit in helping develop children's imagination. Imagination, on the whole, gets rather a bad press among those who deal with children. It is associated with fantasy and falsehood in the minds of too many adults. Children 'imagine' or 'make up' stories to get themselves out of trouble, or let their imaginations run away with them, leading to confusion as to what is real and what is not real. Yet imagination is at the heart of the creativity to which we have just been referring. Imagination is a way of altering our conception of the world, broadening possibilities and opening the way towards change and development. Undoubtedly children must understand the difference between imagination and hard reality, but the tendency to dismiss imagination as at best a trivial exercise in make-believe and at worst as a dangerous path towards falsehood and fantasy is yet another way of denying to children much of their creative potential.

The word 'imagination' (image-ination) refers to the ability to create mental images, but we can also speak of aural imagination. Many composers (Mozart was a prime example) speak of hearing their music, and being required to do little more than write it down. Some poets have also received their poems 'ready-made', and have done little more than alter the occasional line. We can also speak of tactile imagination, in which we imagine ourselves touching or being touched, olfactory imagination in which we imagine smells, and kinaesthetic imagination, in which we imagine body movements of one sort or another. Whether these various forms of imagination are fundamentally different from each others, or different aspects of one mental process, is unclear. But the appropriate development of a lively and self-controlled imagination in children is as important as the development of intelligence and emotional maturity. The imagination needs to be given free expression so that it can be welcomed and acknowledged, and used as a tool which can be called upon almost at will.

In addition to being the inspiration behind the creative arts and much scientific progress, imagination is a powerful means towards self-development. We make extensive use of this in psychotherapy and psychological counselling. For example, when working with children and young people who are anxious about such things as talking in public, taking tests or examinations or visiting the dentist, or who have phobias about things like water or school or particular animals, or who wish to rid themselves of unwanted habits, we help them achieve a relaxed physical state, then encourage them to imagine themselves dealing calmly and easily with whatever it is they find troubling. For example, we will take a student suffering from extreme examination nerves step by step through each of the events leading up to and including the examination itself. Each of these steps, from waking on the examination morning onwards, will be clearly imagined by the student while in a relaxed and confident frame of mind. If feelings of undue anxiety arise we pause, help the student re-establish his or her relaxation and confidence, and then pick up the story again from there.

We help the young smoker to imagine taking a cigarette out of the packet and carrying it towards the mouth while visualizing with repugnance the tar and smoke and other evil substances about to invade the lungs. This feeling of revulsion is held in the mind, and then the smoker is prompted to imagine throwing the unlit cigarette into the wastepaper basket, and feeling immediate self-satisfaction.

The exercise is repeated a number of times over several sessions until it can be carried out successfully with an actual cigarette, and the desire to smoke becomes progressively lessened.

The more clearly the child can imagine feeling calm in the face of the dreaded examination, or experiencing repugnance at the realization of the damage that the cigarette can inflict upon the body, the more effective these exercises are likely to be. People with active imaginations need only a small number of sessions before the desired effect is achieved.

Techniques such as these are well-established both in child and adult psychotherapy, and also form the basis of similar work in hypnotherapy. Interestingly, variants of them have long been used as the basis for spiritual development in many of the great religious traditions of the world. For example, the practitioner is taught to visualize him or herself performing good actions, or to meditate upon a visual image of a god or goddess and then take the divine being down into the heart, where his or her qualities are imagined as arising within the self.

More recently, the value of imagination in helping with the treatment of physical illness has become widely recognized. The sufferer visualizes him or herself regaining the use of injured or otherwise affected parts of the body, or visualizes the immune system fighting off cancer cells or infections. An old saying has it that 'as we think, so we are'. We have a great deal of power to change ourselves in desirable directions simply by imagining that change taking place. The power of the mind to heal – or conversely to predispose us to sickness – is now generally recognized by the medical profession, and it is unfortunate that this power has been long neglected in our materially-minded culture, which teaches us to believe only in the things seen through the outer senses.

VISUALIZATION

Visualization appears to be a particularly effective way of using the imagination. We rarely meet children who pronounce themselves unable to visualize (the condition is more common among adults), and if we do we prove them wrong by asking them if they ever recall their dreams. If the answer is yes, we remind them that dreams are intensely visual experiences – and usually so real that we enter with full belief into the experience, only recognizing it as imaginary when we wake the following morning.

People who have trouble visualizing are typically the victims of an early education that discouraged the ability, and thus prompted it to atrophy. It is rightly said of all the faculties of both mind and body that we must either 'use it or lose it'. Use an ability, whether it be mental or physical, or risk losing it through simple disuse. Respect it, treasure it, and practise it often enough to prevent it from slipping away. This is as true of imagination as it is of the movement of each joint in the physical body. Nature has decreed that we thrive upon activity. If we fail to use one of her gifts, she gets the message that it is unwanted, and takes it away from us.

Think of visualization as a vital tool of the mind, and of meditation as an important way towards the proper recognition and development of this tool. And think of yourself as a facilitator of visualization in your children, and thus of something that will be of enormous practical value to them not only now but throughout their lives. The more children can enjoy and give expression to visualization, the more it will flourish – and the more they will be able to respect it and to recognize its relationship to, and its necessary distinction from, outer reality.

In all the exercises in this chapter, the children should first be asked to establish meditative awareness by concentrating for two or three minutes on their breathing. You can then proceed to the imaginative part of the exercise, but encourage the children to allow the images to form spontaneously in their mind's eye. They should not try to put them there by thinking consciously about what you are saying.

Meditation 11: Meditation for Visualization

The whole of this exercise, including a period for discussion at the end, will probably last around fifteen minutes, but much depends upon you and upon the group. The important thing is to allow sufficient time. It's of little value to tuck meditation sessions into a few odd minutes in between other (perhaps more immediately interesting) activities.

Invite the children to close their eyes and to concentrate upon their breathing for a few moments, then ask them to visualize behind their closed eyelids as follows.

> Visualize the face of someone you admire very much. It may be a sports star, or a pop star, or a friend, or someone in your family. Hold the image steady in your imagination. Remember that it is a picture, so don't let it start moving or talking. Don't get lost in thoughts about this person. Simply keep looking at them. If thoughts come into your head, let them float out again. Don't try too hard to push them away. Just let them come and go of their own accord. Keep your attention focused upon the face in front of you.

Allow the exercise to run for up to five minutes if this seems comfortable. If there are any signs of restlessness (giggling is a common one), say 'just keep the attention clear and focused'. Draw things to a close if the signs of restlessness become too marked. Don't show any indication of annoyance and disappointment if things don't seem to go too well. Remember that you are *offering* meditation to the group, not forcing it upon them. If adolescents get the idea you want them to meditate to please you, or that their restlessness has discomforted you, it becomes much harder to help them develop the appropriate attitude.

Conclude the meditation in the following way.

> Now allow the picture to fade away, so that once more you are looking only at your closed eyelids. Then gently open your eyes and bring your attention back to the room.

Keep the discussion at the end of the meditation relatively short. Especially in the initial stages, a protracted discussion can give children the wrong impression. It is important to get across the concept that meditation is not a big deal. It is simply something we can do in order to help ourselves.

Open the discussion by asking individuals if they were able to keep their attention focused. Don't be drawn into who it was they chose to focus upon. Discuss the process, rather than the details. If nobody offers anything, congratulate the group on their stillness during the meditation, tell them they will have another session like this shortly, and leave it at that. If several people want to talk, hear them out without praising some and neglecting others, then close the discussion by saying that there will be an opportunity for further discussion next time.

Two of the points that are typically raised at this stage are failure to visualize the image, and the image slipping away. In the early stages, some children find that they cannot visualize the image. If this happens, reassure them that we can all visualize. We do it each night in dreams, with such success that while we are asleep we cannot tell dreams from waking life. So all that is needed is practice. One helpful strategy is to look fixedly at an object with the eyes open, then close the eyes suddenly, as if they were the shutters of a camera. The image will then stay in the mind long enough for the meditator to focus upon it.

The image slipping away is another common difficulty with beginners, and again is always overcome with practice. Advise those concerned to bring the image gently back each time it slips away. Counsel them not to try too hard to keep it there. Effort is almost always counter-productive in the early stages of meditation. But they should be alert for the moment when it begins once more to slip away, and should gently bring it back each time. Before long, the mind will get the message, and the image will become stabilized.

Follow-up
You may wish to repeat this technique on several subsequent occasions, especially if the group appears to have difficulty in obtaining and maintaining concentration. A variation is to invite the children to visualize the face again, but then to ask them to narrow their attention to just the eyes, then to the mouth, then to the hair, the ears, and finally to what they think is the most characteristic feature.

Next, invite the children to visualize the whole body, and imagine the person walking – how do they look? Do they give an impression of calm? Of hurry? Of grace? Next, reminding the children to allow the image to arise spontaneously rather than to think about it consciously, ask them what colour best represents the person. Then what geometrical shape. Then what abstract shape. Even children who initially have some difficulty with exercises of this kind usually make rapid progress. The ability is always there. What is needed is the recognition of its importance by the children, together with the opportunity to engage in sufficient practice.

Meditation 12: Aural and Tactile Imagination

Imagination is not just visual. The children can also imagine sounds (aural imagination) and the sense of touch (tactile imagination). Ask the children to imagine certain sounds while in meditation. Don't attempt too many in one session; two or three may be sufficient, and allow enough time for each. You can of course supplement our suggestions with ideas of your own, but any of the following sounds would be suitable.

> A running tap, a kettle boiling, the wind in the trees, a bird singing, a bonfire, a friend's voice, a musical instrument playing a favourite tune, raindrops, a crowd cheering, glass breaking.

A similar exercise can be used for tactile, and indeed olfactory, sensations. The children can be invited to imagine two or three of the following.

> The feel of the wind in their faces as they bicycle, the warm water of a shower, the cool water of a swimming pool, a comfortable bed, sunshine, snowflakes, the pins and needles in a limb 'gone to sleep', the fur of a cat or dog or favourite pet, the pain of a cut knee, a drenching from heavy rain, sand running through the fingers; the taste of a favourite meal, ice cream; the smell of flowers, or hot toast, a fish and chip shop, a polluted city street, hot coffee, frying sausages, new shoes, pages of a book, cola, soap, perfume, fresh bread.

When the children can manage this experience fairly easily, introduce the following visualization.

Meditation 13: Abstract Visualization

This exercise involves replacing faces and everyday objects with abstract images. The reason for moving to abstract shapes is that they are less likely to spark off associations. They therefore induce a calmer mental state, allowing the mind to go deeper into meditation. Abstract shapes can also have an archetypal quality, as if they represent the basic building blocks from which the complex world of form is actually fashioned. Geometrical shapes, such as a circle, best embody this quality. Establish meditative awareness, and then proceed as follows.

In the last session you concentrated upon someone
you admire. This time, you're going to use a
different image. Close your eyes, and once more
direct your attention to your closed eyelids. Now
allow the image of a circle to appear, a white circle
against a red background. Hold the image steadily
in your sight. If it drifts away, bring it gently back.
Notice how big or small the circle is, and whether it
is drawn with a thin or a thick white line. Keep it in
the centre of your awareness. Don't think about the
circle, just observe it. If any thoughts enter your
mind, allow them to float out again. Remember not
to try too hard to push them away. Let them go of
their own accord.

Once you have given these instructions, allow the group to
concentrate in silence. If they become restless, terminate the
session. Otherwise, allow it to run for around five minutes.
End the session by using the form of words given for
Meditation 11.

Follow-up
Discuss the experience of the group afterwards. Could they
see the circle clearly? How did it look? Did they have any
difficulty in remaining focused upon it? If so, what
happened? Did thoughts intrude too much? If so, what kind
of thoughts were they? What were they about? Were they
happy or sad? Why was it that they didn't float away as
hoped?

Sometimes children have difficulty in keeping the circle
abstract. Karen, a ten-year-old, confessed that it kept turning
into a ball, and then she found herself picking it up and
throwing it to one of her friends. A classmate, Ian, found it
turning into a picture of a railway tunnel in a book he'd just
been reading. Tracey complained it kept turning into the face
of a doll, while Mark saw it as the steering wheel in his
mother's car. These associations were natural enough. The

children had clearly got into their heads that things must *mean* something. Their experiences were praised as evidence that they'd stayed with the meditation, but they were encouraged to keep coming back to the abstract circle.

We said earlier that adolescents are engaged in a search for identity, and generally they respond particularly well to any discussion which has to do with the mysteries of their own minds. Make sure that in the discussion you stress from time to time the practical benefits of meditation as a way of going deeper into themselves, and finding out what is there. Allow them also to see how valuable it is to examine their own thoughts. If thoughts intrude or prove troublesome in content, why is this? What does it tell them about the workings of their own minds, and about their preoccupations, concerns, worries, hopes, expectations, excitements and so on?

Unless they have the necessary confidence in each other, children, especially in adolescence, can be rather diffident about talking in front of each other when details of their own thoughts are involved, and it is important to put them at their ease by stressing the need for trust between each other, and emphasizing that no one need feel they should reveal thoughts that they would rather keep to themselves.

Don't let the discussion overstay its welcome. When it's clear that everything has been said, close the discussion and promise another meditation session soon.

Meditation 14: Controlling Visualized Images

As these early sessions are about developing powers of concentration, you can choose a range of shapes on which the group can focus. The children are also developing their powers of visualization, which will prove important to the success of later, more advanced levels of meditation. This technique can be developed in a number of ways, but the following procedure (after establishing the usual state of relaxation, and asking the children to close their eyes) is among the most suitable.

Behind your closed eyelids, see once again the circle that you saw during our last session. Allow the image to establish itself clearly . . . Now allow the circle to grow as large as possible . . . now as small as possible . . . now back to its original size. Now place the circle inside a square. Allow the image to stabilize itself. Now remove the square and put it inside the circle. Now hold the image clearly in your mind. If thoughts arise, remember to let them float out of the mind as easily as they came.

Follow-up
During this and subsequent sessions you can introduce other geometrical shapes such as a triangle and a star. You can also change the background colour from red to green to blue to yellow and back to red again. Or the geometrical shapes can be coloured, and placed upon a white or otherwise contrasting background. Don't allow any of these changes to take place too rapidly, however. Always allow images to be stabilized before they are transformed into other images.

Chapter 10

Finding a Peaceful Place

Many children, even in adolescence, are not fully in touch with their feelings. Sometimes this is because they don't possess the language to explain things properly to themselves, but more often it is because they are caught up in confusion as to what they 'ought' to be feeling. Ask a class of eight-year-old children whether they have any worries, and hardly a hand will go up. Tell them instead that most children of their age have worries, and that you would like to hear about them, and nearly every child in the class will be eager to disclose something. Most of the things disclosed will be genuine, and not merely invented in order to please their teacher.

CHILDREN'S ANXIETIES

Children worry about what their parents and teachers think of them, about their friends or their lack of friends, about their possessions, about their own safety and the safety of the people they love, about being bullied, about their pets, about dying, about where they came from, about God, and even about the state of their health.

In some ways children worry as much as, if not more than, most adults. As the foundations of our mature personalities are largely laid down during childhood, the way in which children deal with their worries can influence much of their coping behaviour throughout life. Children who are helped to keep their anxieties in perspective, and to develop a serenity of mind that prevents them from being overwhelmed by them, are thus advantaged not only in the present but in the years to come.

Meditation helps children deal with anxieties both mentally and physically. The body and the mind are closely linked. If the body is relaxed, it helps the mind to relax. If the body is tense, the mind becomes tense, and a vicious circle develops. If the body is tense, it signals this tension to the mind; the mind tenses in response, which further tenses the body, and the body feeds back yet more anxious signals to the mind. So the process goes on, unless we break the circle by relaxing the body in meditation.

At the same time, meditation helps relieve anxiety by providing the mind with a point of focus. By concentrating upon this point of focus, the mind is less distracted by anxious thoughts. The thoughts may still be there, but the mind does not attend to them, or get caught up in the chain of associations that lead it from one anxiety to another. And as the mind relaxes, so it prompts relaxation in the body.

This can be brought home to children within the context of a general discussion about anxiety. Ask the children what it is like to be anxious. Encourage them to report the physical sensations involved – the pain in the pit of the stomach, the feelings of nausea, the tightness in the shoulders and the neck, the headache. With very young children, it is often helpful to ask them first to imagine a situation in which they feel anxious, and then to report the sensations involved.

Once children are fully aware that anxiety produces bodily reactions, ask them how these can be relieved. Bring out the idea that if the body can 'let go' of these sensations in meditation, by relaxing tight muscles and letting the physical tensions drain away, then the mind is also going to feel more at ease with itself. In addition, the act of meditation, by virtue of its calm non-involvement in thoughts, gives children what can best be described as permission not to dwell on their anxieties. All too often children come to regard anxiety as a merited punishment for their misdeeds and for their weaknesses as human beings. In the minds of many of them, anxiety is inseparably associated with guilt. They are 'bad' boys or girls, and therefore must suffer by feeling guilty about themselves. Meditation helps stop this kind of thinking.

Teaching meditation isn't a way of excusing children's unwanted behaviour. But it is a way of helping them keep things in perspective, so that they can become more rational and less emotional in their self-judgements, and can increase in self-understanding and self-acceptance.

Point out that all the meditation exercises the children have done so far can help relieve anxiety, particularly those in Chapter 5 and those involving concentration upon the breathing and body awareness. These techniques are combined in the following exercise.

Meditation 15: Releasing Anxieties

Remind the children that when concentrating upon their breathing, they should make sure the breath comes from as deep down as possible, that it is calm and regular, and that they attend to it instead of to the thoughts that may be going through their heads. Then ask them to allow their awareness to sweep slowly through their bodies, as in Exercise 9.

> If you find any tension in any muscle or group of muscles, gently let it go. Check particularly the muscles of your back, your stomach, your shoulders, your neck, and the muscles of the face. Notice how letting go of tensions in the body helps you let go of any tensions in the mind. Now bring your awareness to your breathing, and keep it there. Should any worries or anxieties come into your mind, let them go in the same way that you let go the tensions in the muscles.

In addition, an excellent way of helping the mind to relax

when faced with particular anxieties is to use the method employed by Fiona in Chapter 8, namely to visualize a peaceful place, and allow oneself to enter and enjoy its serenity. Most children tend to choose the seaside, or somewhere in the country, or a park, or a quiet room all to themselves. Some children, however, prefer the excitement of a funfair or a theme park. The important thing is that it should be the child's own choice, and that they should feel happy with it.

SELF-EMPOWERMENT

A further benefit of meditation, as we stress particularly in Chapter 5 but also elsewhere, is the ability to deal with personal feelings instead of being at the mercy of them. This is an important aspect of self-empowerment. From childhood onwards, we need to feel in charge of our lives, rather than feeling at the mercy of the guilt, the self-accusations, the low self-esteem and the other dark energies that can come between us and happiness. Anxiety, as much as anything, is a habit – a habit all too often acquired early in life and arising from the feeling that we don't deserve to be happy. So when happiness appears, the mind automatically hunts around for reasons why we should not be happy. And obligingly, something we 'ought' to be worrying about rises to the surface.

Anxiety has a legitimate role to play even in childhood, in that it warns children of dangers, reminds them of things needing attention, prompts them to reflect upon the consequences of their behaviour, and prods them when they have failed to live up to the reasonable expectations others may have of them. But it should be a valued servant and not a demanding master.

When discussing the role of meditation in self-empowerment, it is helpful to ask children what happens to their thoughts when they are anxious. Allow them to recognize that at such times thoughts often seem to take on a life of their own, one thought leading to another leading to another and so on until the mind embarks upon a mental roller-coaster of vain imaginings.

Children often readily recognize that the mind plays the 'what if?' game. ('What if this happened, and what if this led to that, and that led to something else?') The 'what if' game is typically followed by the 'how would?' game. ('How would my parents/teachers/friends feel if these things happened? How would I feel? How would I get out of the situation in which I landed myself? How would I get back on the right side of my parents/teachers/friends? How would I make sure that such awful things never happened again? How would I get back to feeling happy once more?' And so on.)

The great American writer Mark Twain once said that his life had been full of tragedies, and most of them never happened. The creative power of the mind, of so much value in other contexts, is a past master at dredging up the most far-fetched things to worry about once it embarks upon its roller-coaster. It has the knack of making the most implausible things seem plausible, even inevitable. For some children, virtually every possible tragic event in the world is waiting to pounce upon them around the very next corner.

The way for them to avoid the roller-coaster is to keep their minds focused upon the things they want to think. If their anxieties are illusory, then they must refuse to become caught up in them. If their anxieties are real, then they must concentrate upon seeing if solutions exist. Meditation not only calms the mind, it opens it to the creative thinking that helps produce these solutions. Explain to children that meditation is similar to riding a bicycle. When riding a bicycle, they have to keep the front wheel pointing ahead. If they lose control and let it wander to one side, the bicycle will career off the road, with disaster as the inevitable result. Most children understand analogies of this kind.

Another useful exercise is to ask them to focus upon their breathing while you clap your hands at random intervals. The claps represent anxious thoughts, and most children will recognize that if their minds are calmly centred, they are not as startled or distracted by the clapping as they would otherwise be.

Children are in the process of learning how their minds work. Much of the mind is still a mystery to them. They are unaware of its potential. Thus to be told that the mind has the power to direct and shape itself, rather than be at the mercy of any emotion or feeling that chooses to surface, can in itself be a liberating experience. It allows them to push forward the boundaries of the known, and in the case of many children introduces them to an enduring interest in the workings and the possibilities of their own inner world.

Chapter 11

Meditation for Moral and Spiritual Growth

THE DECLINE IN VALUES

We live in times of rapid social change, in which the nature of right and wrong is becoming increasingly blurred. Equally importantly, the decline in religious belief and practice has left people doubtful about their own natures, and unsure of the importance of traditional values such as compassion, love, generosity, and a belief in a divine being and in an eternal soul that survives the death of the physical body. The result is that children are often given insufficient guidance as to how they should live their lives, and how they should think about their own being.

Meditation has been at the heart of all the great spiritual traditions. Hinduism, Buddhism, Islam, Judaism, Sikhism and Jainism have all emphasized the importance of meditation from childhood onwards, and although Christianity has tended to rely more upon prayer and divine ritual, meditation has also featured strongly in some of its denominations, and is currently reclaiming attention in several more. There are many reasons for this link between meditation and spirituality.

Stilling the mind leads to peace

The stilling of the mind that occurs in meditation helps the meditator listen to the subtle promptings that come from the deeper levels of awareness. These promptings are almost invariably to do with feelings of warmth, love and acceptance towards the self and others. Regular meditators are almost always peaceful people.

The deepest nature of both child and adult is caring, benevolent and loving. It is largely life circumstances that lead to anger, fear and ultimately violence. Meditation puts the mind more in touch with this deeper nature, and helps both child and adult to express it more freely in the world.

Meditation puts materiality into perspective

Much of the unrest and squabbling that take place in children's lives, as in those of adults, is to do with material possessions. Children live in a materialistic world, and want the things that others have. The lesson that true happiness comes from within rather than from material goods is one that is difficult to teach, and one that is often only learned as a result of bitter experience.

Meditation helps children sit quietly with themselves, and to discover resources and positive feelings about themselves that are worth much more than the transient, temporary pleasures that material objects can bring. Through their experience of meditation, many children become more self-aware and self-sufficient. They tend to demand less, and to enjoy a more realistic and balanced presence in the world, a presence which is an important part of spirituality.

Meditation can be directed towards spiritual themes

Meditation can be directed towards what many would regard as specifically spiritual themes, as shown in Meditation 16 (p. 105). Thus after concentrating for a short time upon the breath, the children can be asked to focus upon feelings of gentleness and peace, upon compassion and love for others, and upon a sense of their own value as living beings.

This will not turn them into unrealistically pacific creatures, unable to deal with the hard knocks of the world. On the contrary, they are often better able to handle such things because they see beyond the pains and disappointments of the moment. They become equipped to take a more objective and understanding view of their own needs and of the needs of others, and to take calmer, more informed and less selfish decisions.

In some cases, as meditation goes deeper, children may experience a hint of those mystical states which put one in touch with what is variously called cosmic consciousness, God or the divine, which appears to be the ground of our being, the source of our lives.

At such moments there is a sense of unity with all existence. The barriers between themselves and the rest of creation become less rigid. They understand that the gift of life is shared with one another, and with the animals, plants, and all the wonders of creation. Such experiences increase a child's tolerance and openness, and help develop a compassion which is not forced, but which comes from a true realization of the inter-connectedness and the inter-dependency of all things.

GIVING AND RECEIVING AFFECTION

Children are born with a tremendous capacity to give and receive affection, and to feel compassion for the suffering of others. This capacity stems not just from an instinct impelling them to cling to those who feed and care for them. Watch a very young child dissolve into tears if they see another child in distress. Notice how ready they are to join in with the laughter of others, even if the cause of this laughter is beyond their understanding. Observe the care they lavish upon their pets and other animals, and the concern with which they attend to imaginary hurts suffered by their dolls and other toys. Children have an inborn capacity for empathy, for reaching out emotionally to others and sharing in their feelings. They are born, in a real sense, to love and be loved.

As children grow older, the spontaneous affection with which they greet the world gradually becomes overlaid by experience. They find out that others are not always loving towards them, that people will take advantage of their natural generosity and willingness to share, that others will not always reciprocate their generosity, that far too many people live their lives through competition rather than co-operation. The world is indeed at times a hard and unforgiving place, ready to exploit innocence and good nature. But this is no reason for children to repress their own positive feelings, or to view the world outside the immediate circle of family and friends with suspicion, or to take advantage of others in the way that others may take advantage of them.

The following meditation is designed to help children keep alive, in a realistic and responsible way, their ability to feel unselfish love for those who treat them less than well, and even for those they have never met.

Meditation 16: Love and Compassion

Start by helping the children to re-establish the peaceful experience reached at the end of Meditation 15. This doesn't involve *asking* them to re-establish it. Experiences in meditation rarely come directly to order. Instead, go through Meditation 15 step by step once more (though rather more quickly than before), taking care not to remind the children how they felt the first time.

> Now as you experience this sense of being just who you are, let yourself feel love and acceptance for yourself. You are who you are, and you are happy to be who you are.
>
> Become aware of sharing this loving spirit with the people you care for most in the world, your

parents and your brothers and sisters and perhaps
your grandparents. Let your love for these people
and their love for you flow between you. Be aware
of its warmth and its caring.

Now extend this flow of love until it includes
your best friends. Visualize them in your
imagination if you like, and feel your love for them
and their love for you enfolding you like a warm
embrace.

Now allow this love to flow between you and the
friends you know less well . . . now between you
and the people you know but who are not yet your
friends, the people you meet occasionally or who
live near you.

Now let the love flow wider still, to touch those
people you may not like very much, those people
perhaps you feel rather angry with, those
people who maybe have not treated you very well.
Feel how pleasant and healing this love is, taking
away any negative emotions, any hostility or fear.

Now go further, and allow your love to flow out
to people you've never met, to people up and down
the country . . . now to people abroad, and
particularly those who are suffering and unhappy,
those who are short of food or clean water, or who
are sick, or who are threatened by war or violence
or by natural disasters like storms or floods or
famine. Feel that these people are human beings just
like us, and that they suffer in the same way that
you would suffer if you were living where they are
living, and if you had to experience what they
are experiencing.

This meditation is based upon a very old Buddhist loving-
kindness meditation which, used regularly, is said to release
the meditator's full potential for compassion and empathy. It
can be used in connection with animals as well as humans,
firstly any pets the children may have, then their favourite

animals, then the animals towards which they feel neutral, and from there to the animals which they may actively dislike. In the same way it can be used to arouse increased care and concern for the environment, developing from things near at hand like flowers and trees, to rivers and mountains, to forests and oceans. In each case the purpose is the same, to help children feel more in touch with the objects of the natural world, and to feel something of the respect and love which will lead them to cherish the environment.

Often an exercise of this kind leads to immediate practical results. Children not only tend to be more friendly and understanding towards each other, they also take more interest in good causes, and often ask if they can write letters as a group to influential people urging action over some injustice which they have identified. These responses are not just a temporary phenomenon. With each experience of the meditation, children find greater potential within themselves for warmth, understanding and charity. Many of the apparently cruel actions of children, such as bullying, arise from lack of opportunity to experience what is best in themselves. Meditation sessions, in which children are allowed to access their own feelings, are often of far more immediate and lasting value than any number of lectures on the need to be kinder towards each other.

CONTACT WITH NATURE

Although we are in contact with nature every moment of our lives, the problem is that for most of the time we just aren't aware of it. Our bodies are in contact with the atmosphere, with the material of our clothes, with the ground under our feet. Our lungs are in contact with the air, constantly taking from and giving back to nature. Our stomachs are in contact with food and water, and each of our senses is potentially taking in nature in all her beauty. We evolved, over the aeons, in intimate contact with nature, dependent upon her for our sustenance, for our warmth, for our safety, for our very existence. In view of this close relationship, we have a psychological need for contact with nature. We are unlikely to be truly at ease for long if we are cut off from her soothing presence. In the modern world, children are increasingly surrounded by man-made objects and artificial materials. Even the water they drink comes from springs and rivers which they may never see, while the central heating that warms their homes is fed by flames they rarely witness. They live enclosed in concrete walls, eat processed, denatured foods, drink concoctions full of artificial colourings and flavourings, breath air polluted with the dust and dirt of modern living, and are entertained by watching artificial people acting out artificial dramas in an artificial medium projected upon a harmfully radioactive screen. They are dosed with antibiotics, and fed with microwaved food. They travel even short distances to school in tin boxes, cut off from the wind and the rain and the sunshine. They sit on furniture manufactured from plastics, and wear clothes made from synthetics. They eat fruit and vegetables grown with artificial fertilizers and doused with artificial insecticides; their bodies are rarely given the exercise which they need to keep healthy, or fed with a sensible diet.

Small wonder then that less and less of their lives are lived as nature intended, in harmony with her healing grace. Meditation helps children to rediscover something of their roots, and to rediscover the ancient magic of the earth from which their bodies spring. The specific practices to help this process are given in Meditation 16, but again just being still is a move in the right direction. In stillness children can tune in to the beating of their hearts, to the faint but unmistakable sound made by the blood as it moves through their arteries and veins, and to the manifold sounds arising from the world around them – the creaking of chairs and desks, the wind and the rain on the windows, the barking of dogs, the song of the birds, the murmur of voices in the corridor outside, even the rumble of traffic. Each sound is attended to, but not labelled and held onto by the mind. Sounds are thus heard *as sounds*. If the eyes are opened and visual impressions taken in, they are taken in as visual impressions, and again not labelled.

For all their value at certain times, labels can come between the mind and direct experience. As soon as children learn to label, they are made to feel they have explained whatever it is they are hearing or seeing. The label demystifies things. The sound is *only* the wind in the trees, *only* the water in the stream, *only* the song of the birds, *only* the murmur of voices. In meditation, children can be gently prompted to avoid the trap of labels, and even to avoid holding on to what is heard and what is seen. Once something has been heard and seen, it is allowed to return once more to the background, while another sensation moves into awareness and takes its place.

Putting children more closely in touch with nature through meditation is not only of benefit to their psychological health, it prepares them for the task of taking better care of their environment. If children are helped to respond to the natural world with sensitivity and proper awareness, they develop a feeling of kinship for her beauty and vulnerability, and they experience personal hurt if she is harmed. They have no wish to destroy the things they have learned to love. Because of the freshness with which they see the world, children, and particularly young children, are innately closer to nature than are adults. Meditation helps to maintain and deepen this closeness, and the thought of wantonly despoiling the beauty which still exists all around becomes unthinkable to them.

PART 3

The Practicalities of Teaching Meditation

Chapter 12

The Practicalities of Meditation with Children

It is probably hard to imagine lively young children sitting still with their eyes closed, and enjoying it, and it would be fair to say that it does not come naturally to most of them. Indeed, not all children will take to it; as with adults, it suits some more than others. However, it is important to give children the opportunity to experience meditation and its related activities, creating the conditions which are optimum for them within the constraints of whatever environment they may be in.

This section of the book considers the practical application of some of the activities we have been discussing, at school and at home, beginning with children at the lower end of the age range and continuing into young adulthood. Each chapter contains practical advice on the practice of meditation and its related activities in three different situations:

- at school, with a small group of about nine children
- at school, with the whole class
- at home where you might work with one or two children, or with the whole family together.

Detailed guidance will be given, including how to introduce meditation to the children, and strategies for encouraging co-operative behaviour.

It might sometimes seem that there is more detail and explanation than necessary, particularly for experienced teachers. This is partly because, as explained in the introduction, this book is written for a wider readership which includes adults who are relatively unused to working with children. We also anticipate that many readers will not read the book sequentially so we have tried, as far as possible, to make the instructions in each chapter fairly self-contained (which explains a certain amount of repetition). We, hope, therefore, that experienced teachers will bear with us if some of the directions or explanations seem overly detailed.

It is important to remember that these are only guidelines and you might find that for you and your class, or your particular home situation, other strategies and methods might be more effective. Each child or group of children may have different capabilities and preferences. You should therefore see this section of the book as a basis for your own work, and remain ever alert to the children's responses and needs, always open to suggestions for new inventive ways of approaching the activities in an effort to find out which ones best suit them.

PREPARING YOURSELF FOR MEDITATION WITH CHILDREN

Practice

It is important that whichever age group you are leading, whether at home or in school, you practise the exercises yourself several times *before* introducing them to the children, so that you feel confident in what you are doing. Your own experience should also help to give you insight into some of the joys and difficulties of meditation. This in turn will help you to empathize with the children and enable you to pre-empt potential problems by finding possible solutions from your own experience.

If, after using any of the exercises in this book several times, you find that you do not enjoy them or are not comfortable with them, then you should not attempt to teach them. Your state of mind, attitude and positive energy is crucial to the success of the activities and to the well-being of the children as well as to yourself. It is also important that you are sensitive to the children's moods and are prepared to change and adapt the session accordingly. If only a small part of the session seems to be meditation proper, do not be concerned. With perseverance, this will increase as long as the children like being in the session and relate well to you, and, of course, as long as you also enjoy the session.

Centre yourself

Before leading any meditation or related activity, it is beneficial for both you and the children if you, personally, take a moment or two to centre yourself. If you are a teacher, you do not have to build this in to your timetable or take time away from the class. Centring yourself can be done simply and easily in any situation. Allowing yourself a few minutes to sit quietly, and to relax and focus on your breathing is ideal, but the practicalities of, for example, teaching in a busy school make it unlikely that you will able to offer yourself this luxury. Instead, briefly turn your mind inwards wherever you are, whether you are standing or sitting, and relax your body. To do this, just direct your attention from your feet upwards until your whole body feels relaxed. With practice, you will be able to do this almost instantaneously. Direct your consciousness to your relaxed body while you take three or four calming breaths. This should enable you to feel sufficiently at one with yourself to begin the meditation.

Establishing trust

Meditation and its related exercises encourage a deal of self-disclosure in the form of speaking, writing or drawing. It is therefore crucial that you build up trust with the children with whom you work. This trust should enable the children to feel safe in anything which they disclose about themselves, whether it be at school or at home. It should be made explicit that whatever is said during these sessions remains within the domain of the group, or between you and your child at home, and will not be used in any negative way at any other time. It cannot be emphasized enough that it is absolutely crucial to the success of this work that everyone feels and knows that they are completely safe.

MEDITATION AT SCHOOL

Meditation and its related activities are not yet commonly accepted in schools as part of the curriculum, so if you decide to spend a substantial amount of time on teaching them during the school day or, in the case of older children, offer them as extra-curricular activities, it is important that other members of staff understand what is going on and, if necessary, approve. As we said in the introduction to this book, it is vital that the necessary permission and co-operation of the school, and where appropriate parents, is obtained for work of this kind.

When to meditate in school

Ideally meditation should be incorporated into the whole school ethos, although it need not be referred to as 'meditation'. It could just as well be seen as an activity for stress-reduction, relaxation and concentration. If this were normal practice for one or two minutes at the beginning and end of every session, its calming effect would permeate the whole school. The school would soon develop a calm, relaxed, organized and productive atmosphere.

Meditation and its related exercises may be carried out with the whole class under the guidance of their own teacher. Alternatively, a smaller group may be taken out of the classroom and led either by their own teacher while the rest of the class is engaged in another activity, or by a different teacher. As with most other subjects, it is important that children enjoy the activity and respect and enjoy being with the teacher who leads it.

If you are the class teacher, you will already have developed a good relationship with the class, know the children well, be alert to their responses, and have established good discipline. On the other hand, if you are not the class teacher and thus have a different relationship with the children, they might see meditation as a treat because it is outside the normal routine, and different from anything else they will have done. There is always a freshness in being with a different teacher.

After several sessions, meditation should become optional, but all the children will need to experience meditation and its related activities before they can decide whether or not they wish to continue. If the sessions are organized so that small groups are taken out of class for meditation, this should not coincide with a period when the rest of the children are doing something which those in the meditation group would much rather be doing. This would make them resentful and agitated, and the meditation exercises might become construed as a chore or even a punishment.

If you are to work with the whole class, which can be very effective, then it is preferable initially to do so at the same time every day, ideally twice or three times a day. It need take only a few minutes. For example, it would be a good way to begin and end each morning and afternoon.

MEDITATION AT HOME

If you are a parent or carer, you may want to try meditation at home with your child or children. How they respond will depend to a large extent on your relationship with them. Many parents experience their children as less compliant at home than at school. This may be because home is where children feel able to let themselves go, to be themselves, to have moods and to express themselves as they wish, whereas school demands a certain level of conformity and co-operation.

If you tend to share activities with your children – such as reading, playing, writing, drawing and making things together – introducing meditation will be easier for you. Even so, at first meditation seems such a novel activity that it is easy for children to feel embarrassed and self-conscious. It is therefore particularly important that you feel comfortable with the activity yourself; if you feel at all awkward, you will convey this to your children.

It might be that others in the family would like to take part, which would certainly be beneficial for the family both as a group and as individuals. Meditation is a very rewarding activity to share together. For the benefit of young children, the session should be short, but parent(s) and older children can continue later for a longer period.

WHAT CAN BE ACHIEVED?

We have explained the far-reaching benefits of meditation with children, but these are not always evident straight away. Concentrate upon the immediate advantages. Meditation gives you a space to spend 'quality time' with your children which you might otherwise not have found, and in this way it can help you to understand each other better, thereby further enhancing your relationship. Whether you are a parent, carer or teacher, the calmer and more centred behaviour which your children will express as a result of the exercises in this book will make life more harmonious for everyone.

This may sound idyllic and may not reflect your first experiences of meditation with your children. Do not worry; all new learning has its ups and downs. The more you practise with your children, the easier it will become. Speaking from our personal experience, these quiet moments can help to transform your day.

It should be emphasized that although we suggest exercises for particular age groups, children vary enormously in their individual characteristics and aptitudes. Activities which some four-year-olds may be able to do may be less readily accepted by older children. The ages we have suggested are only guidelines. As we emphasize throughout the book: you are the best judge of what will suit the particular children with whom you intend to work.

The important rule is always to remain positive, and expect the best from the children. Sometimes what they can achieve is very surprising. We have seen children considered as 'disruptive' take very well to these exercises, and quieter children less well. You should aim to give all the children in your care the experience of the different activities in a positive and safe environment, with plenty of encouragement. If they find some of the exercises difficult, help them to persevere. If they do not like particular exercises, do not worry; it is likely that they will enjoy others and then may gradually take to the original exercises in their own time.

WHAT IF THE CHILDREN DO NOT ENJOY MEDITATION?

If after several attempts to help your children with meditation and the related activities, they are still not interested or if you find it hard to come to grips with it yourself, leave it for a while and try again a little later. Some children may never take to it and forcing them would be an unhelpful thing to do. Do not be disappointed if your attempts are not initially successful: all is not lost. There are other ways of achieving the same results.

As you will have seen in Chapter 1, the benefits of meditation and the related activities include an increase in sensitivity to others and to nature, and in self-understanding. Meditation can enhance children's capacity for love and compassion, and improve their self-esteem and relationships.

However, you can help them with these things in your everyday activities without any special techniques or exercises. It it sadly often forgotten that children learn more from the example of people they care about, admire and would like to identify with, than in any other way. If your children are very young, take them for walks, and admire the flowers, the trees and the grass with them. Enjoy the different weathers and look for the positive in every situation. No matter how bad things might seem on occasions, there is always something to be gained from any situation. Demonstrate your respect for all forms of life. Show your love of animals by your appreciation and care for them. Simple things such as putting spiders and other insects out into the garden instead of killing them will also help children to understand the sanctity of life. Look for positive qualities and actions in your children that you can praise, rather than draw attention to their failings.

If they do something which you can see will have negative consequences, either for them or for others around them, you will, of course, need to alert them to this and suggest better ways of handling the situation, but be as patient as you can, and explain matters in a language that they can follow. If someone is unkind to them at school, talk to them about it, show that you understand how they feel and explain that when people get angry or are unkind it often means that they too are unhappy inside. Explain to them that doing good and kind things will bring good things to them. Talk from your own experience of life. This will enhance their understanding and tolerance of others as well as their compassion. In turn, your understanding and wisdom will also enhance their self-understanding, their self-esteem and their relationships with others.

If you can do all these things with them, your children will feel understood and loved. If they are shown love, tolerance, understanding and forgiveness, they will learn to show these qualities to others. Their self-confidence and sense of identity will strengthen as they learn to understand and love the world around them. These are the greatest gifts you can give them; they will provide the children with strength and support for the rest of their lives.

Chapter 13

Beginning Meditation with Five- to Eight-Year-Olds

One of the main characteristics of children of this age group is their short span of concentration. Often they are easily distracted and quickly become restless if they do not feel fully engaged in what they are doing. Working successfully with this age group requires, therefore, a relatively short period of time spent on each of the the activities and as much variety as possible. The more you work with the children and learn about their preferences, their responses and their capabilities, the easier it will become to tailor your programme of meditation exercises specifically to them. Children of this age are usually very receptive to new things, and if they like you, they will generally try really hard in whatever they do with you, as much to please you as themselves.

The advantages of meditation have been discussed throughout the book. Starting to meditate at such an early age can set a strong foundation for later work of this kind and can help children to begin to improve the quality of their life.

MEDITATION WITH SMALL GROUPS

We will begin with the practicalities of taking a group of five- to eight-year-old children out of the class into another room, say two or three times a week. A group of between five and nine children is optimum.

Time

The actual time spent in meditation will be quite short at first, one minute at the most. But the activities in preparation for it and related to it will occupy between ten and fifteen minutes, depending on how many of the activities you decide to do. Remember that time needs to be allowed for getting to the room used for the meditation activities, taking off shoes and putting them on (which can take much longer, taking into account the problem of tying laces).

Selecting your group

It can be a temptation when choosing a group of children for this activity, to select only the ones whom you are sure will behave sensibly and who are most likely to sit still. One reason for this is that you might feel that over-boisterous children would only disrupt the good ones, making the activity more difficult for everyone, including yourself. This is a decision which rests with you, but it is worth considering that it is perhaps the more restless children who could most benefit from both the exercises and the small group attention which the activity offers.

The room

Ideally the children should always be taken to the same room, and preferably always at the same time of day. Young children tend to respond well to routine and predictability. If possible, the room should not be too bright, nor too gloomy. The temperature should be such that the children are neither too hot nor too cold. There should be as few distractions as possible (for example, no interesting toys within easy reach!). If the room happens to face onto a playground, then curtains or blinds will minimize distraction, and will help to avoid self-consciousness if other children gaze in curiously at the group.

Very gentle music playing softly as the children come into the room will also aid relaxation. In fact it is sometimes helpful if the music is played throughout the session. It should be very soft, with a slow even tempo all the way through. A 'New Age' tape or CD would be ideal. The room should preferably be empty of furniture, or at least have a large space in the middle where children can sit comfortably in a circle. If the floor is carpeted, all the better. If the floor is hard and cold, then chairs may be used, but make sure they are easy to move about, since there will be movement around the room at some point in the session.

Beginning the session

The session really begins as soon as the children are collected from their class. They should be encouraged to walk into the meditation room quietly and, once in the room, to take off their shoes in silence and sit in a circle. This works best if you can sit in the circle yourself as soon as possible so that they can join you. Be particularly patient with the children in the early sessions and never raise your voice. Speak to them clearly and firmly. Initially, some of the very lively ones will find walking into a big space and sitting quietly too much of an effort, and they may rush into the room, fling their shoes anywhere and promptly run around the room before coming to the circle. Don't let that put you off; the behaviour is usually due to natural high spirits, combined with novelty and a big space in which to move around. These livelier children may also be testing out the rules in a new situation. Gradually, as they get used to this new event, this will change. We have noticed that after a few sessions children tend to quieten down, line up their shoes neatly without being asked and take their places without fuss.

Once in the circle, some children may try to engage the attention of either you or the other children; they may make a noise or deliberately tease another child. This is where you take a gentle but firm stand and explain the rules of the session to the children. It is important for them to learn to respect others' space and wishes. Explain the strategy of 'self-controlled exclusion' as described below, which is in the interest of all members of the group. 'Self-controlled exclusion' is an effective strategy for dealing with disruptive behaviour in any group situation, but which allows the disruptive child to retain his or her freedom of choice about whether they take part in the lesson or not.

Self-controlled exclusion

If a disruptive child does not respond to your firm but gentle efforts to ask him or her to sit quietly, a very effective strategy is that of self-controlled exclusion. He or she should be asked to leave the circle. Explain that it is because they are disturbing people who would like to continue with the activity, and who do not wish to be disturbed. Ask the child to sit facing the wall away from the group until he or she feels able to join in again without disrupting the group. If the errant children sit out facing the group, they tend to make even greater efforts to attract everyone's attention by rolling around or making faces etc. Even with their backs to the group, they may start to make funny noises. If the noises persist, the child concerned should be warned that he or she will be asked to go back to their classroom. If this doesn't help, then you will have to carry out your decision and send them back to their class. This is often upsetting for them and therefore for you, but in our experience this happens only once. As soon as the children are sure that you mean what you say and see that you give them every chance to stay in the group, they tend to settle down. It is important that this removal from the group is not seen as a punishment. It should be seen as simply protecting the interests of the group activity and as a rejection of the behaviour and not of the child.

Of course, it will feel like a punishment to the child at first, but if you have explained carefully the reason why it has to be done, and make it clear that whether or not they join in the group activities is entirely within their control, they will eventually develop a sense of responsibility for themselves and for the other group members. Always be pleased for them to come back into the group of their own accord and carry on from that point as before, expecting the best from them. If you do this, the children will feel less at the mercy of your judgement. This is crucial; you are allowing the children to retain their personal power and take responsibility for themselves. They have complete control over whether to sit in the group or to face the wall. This avoids feelings of rejection, and helps children to develop a sense of responsibility towards others. Treated in this way, children are able to recognize the effects of their actions and realize their own efficacy. Most children generally like to be part of anything interesting which is going on, and before long settle down and naturally return to the group. What frequently happens is that disruptive children soon learn to leave and return to the circle of their own accord, maybe out of respect for the group or perhaps to continue testing their own autonomy. An instance in my own [Ingrid's] experience which demonstrates the use of 'self-controlled exclusion' is recorded below.

Darren

When I was a young teacher, a six-year-old child in my class had a lot of personal problems which resulted in particularly disruptive behaviour, frequently throwing violent temper tantrums, hurling furniture around and screaming. He was a very low achiever and always seemed to be angry and upset. I used the above technique with him (combined with others described below), asking him to sit behind the blackboard until he was ready to come out. It was very hard at first and very tempting to give in to him. The first time I tried this technique, it became quiet behind the blackboard so I looked over the top and saw him sitting on a chair curled up rocking to and fro. It was all I could do not to go round and hold him in my arms. Using all my strength, I resisted. After a while his little head peered around the blackboard and he sidled over to his seat. He picked up his reading book, which he couldn't read and held it upside down in front of his face, which was now pink. Resisting all urges to make a huge fuss of him, I brought him quickly into the class 'chat' which was a common daily activity. He responded well and I had the opportunity to praise him and show him our appreciation that he was back among us. It was important that the other children responded in the same way and they did. It was not long before the time behind the blackboard was reduced considerably, his work improved dramatically, and eventually I never had to ask him to go there. I noticed that if Darren began to feel disruptive, he would just walk around the blackboard of his own accord, emerge immediately from the other side, return to his place and carry on with his work. That, combined with keeping him busy, recognizing his efforts and praising all the good things about him, so that he felt respected and loved, helped him to rise to near the top of the class in most of his subjects. He was allowed to shine.

Having to sit out could happen a few times to some children in your early meditation sessions, but it has very quick positive results. One reason for its effectiveness may be that the other children approve of it. They see it as fair because the responsibility lies in the child's own hands. So this practice is beneficial not only for the errant child but also for the rest of the group. Through this they learn not only to take responsibility for themselves but that angry punishment is not the most constructive way to deal with people who do not always conform to our accepted standards.

Using up excess energy
If the children have spent most of the time before the meditation session sitting quietly and seem a bit restless, then it is a good idea for them to engage in a short exercise before you start. This could be simply stretching as high as they can, on their toes, arms upwards, trying to reach the ceiling or the sky, then as wide as they can, trying to touch the walls on each side of the room with their arms outstretched, fingers

reaching, and their legs stretched wide apart. They usually put considerable effort into this, and may be quite out of breath afterwards. This might then be followed by a systematic shaking of first one hand and arm, then the other, followed by each leg and foot, then finally the whole body so that they feel loose and relaxed. They should then organize themselves quietly into the circle ready for the next part of the session.

Communication (the 'chat')

Before beginning the first meditation exercise, a good way to proceed is to allow each child to have the opportunity to say how he or she is feeling now. This allows the children to talk about their worries, hopes or fears, to feel safe, accepted and therefore more settled. Initially with this age group of five- to eight-year-olds, you may find that the range of emotions which they describe is limited to happy and sad, with maybe a reference or two to being excited. This is fine; the range will increase naturally as the children develop their capacity for introspection and learn to understand their own emotions. The function of this 'chat' is to help to increase the children's emotional awareness, as well as helping them learn to empathize with others. Allow a little time for gentle exploration of issues with them, but if they choose not to enlarge upon things, let it go. In this way children learn how to listen, how best to respond and how to express themselves. They learn very quickly not to interrupt each other and often reveal a caring side of their nature which may have gone hitherto unnoticed or misinterpreted. An example of this is illustrated by the case of Michael below.

Michael

Eight-year-old Michael was always getting into trouble. He would get into quarrels with other children, often ending up with some form of physical aggression, yet there was something very lovable about him. During our pre-meditation chat one of the children in the group, Sharon, said that she was sad because she couldn't go to visit her aunty. Michael retorted, 'Huh, that's not awful.' Sharon was hurt at this remark and she and the other group members were cross with Michael. They told him off and he got upset because he couldn't understand what was wrong. Normally this situation would have escalated into a full scale confrontation. I [Ingrid] was able to interject and ask Michael what had prompted him to say that. He replied, 'I didn't mean to upset her, I just didn't think it really mattered.' This gave me the space to explain that different things are upsetting to different people and that even if we wouldn't feel the same as they would in a situation it is more helpful if we try to understand them, or at least to accept that they are upset. He seemed satisfied with this and voluntarily said sorry to Sharon. Thereafter he was quite different in our 'chat' part of the session and proved to be a sensitive and caring child. He had misunderstood and had in turn been misunderstood himself. He had been attacked, his natural defence was to counterattack, then war would break out. This session had given everyone an opportunity to develop a greater understanding and therefore tolerance of one another.

You will generally find that children enjoy this part of the session, and they will soon remind you if you forget to include it at the beginning. It seems to settle them, and allows them to feel accepted and understood. You may wish to develop this part of this session into another kind of related activity outside the meditation group.

Movement meditation

After the 'chat' or sharing part of the activity, you may wish to introduce a movement activity, especially if there was no initial 'loosening-up' exercise. Asking the children to walk slowly around the room quietly without bumping into each other, and changing direction at your bidding is a good way to start (an early version of the kinhin we mention in Chapter 7). When they are competent at this, increase the speed, but they should still be walking quietly and avoiding contact with anyone else. If they seem to handle this well, ask them to walk backwards, looking over their shoulders, first slowly then a little more quickly. This exercise encourages concentration, alertness, co-ordination and self-discipline.

The growing seed

Another successful preliminary exercise which teaches concentration, imagination, co-ordination and grace, is the 'growing seed'. Ask the children to find a space in the room and curl up into a little ball. Join in with them, saying something like the following.

> You are a tiny seed in the ground covered with earth. It's lovely and warm and you feel the soft earth all around you. You have felt the gentle rain, and now you feel the warm sun shining on the earth. You start to grow . . . very slowly until you are poking through the ground. You keep growing and your leaves start to unfurl, maybe one opens before the others, you grow up, up and up, you see the sun smiling down upon you, you feel its warmth, and you stretch as tall as you can to reach it. You feel the warmth on your face . . . the day passes and the sun slowly disappears and you slowly begin to curl up again until you are a tiny little ball again.

Children appreciate it if the teacher joins in with them, as long as she or he keeps watching them all the time. Don't forget to praise them collectively at the end. Children usually try very hard with this exercise and tend to enjoy it. Below is a small example of the kind of effect this exercise can have on the young children doing it:

Julie

During the above exercise Julie, a five-year-old girl, said, 'Oh, that was lovely, can we do it again with our eyes closed?' The children thought this was a good idea and tried very hard. They enjoyed it immensely and used a lot of control to move slowly and gracefully, opening out as if into a tall plant. Some wanted to be sunflowers and some tulips, while others wanted to be a tree. Then Julie had another request: 'Can we do it again with love in our hearts?' From this it would seem that the work touched something quite deep in some of the children. The children were very amenable to this but one little boy looked puzzled and asked, 'How do you do it with love in your heart?' I [Ingrid] suggested, 'Think of the person you like best in the world, and imagine them coming towards you smiling. Think how you feel about them, how happy you are when they are around you and how you care about whether they are happy or sad. That is probably the feeling of love in your heart.' This seemed enough guidance to satisfy him.

Getting ready for sitting meditation

Begin by asking the children to sit up straight without straining. Sitting cross-legged on the floor is generally the most comfortable way. If some of them find that this is not comfortable, allow them to discover their own way, but tell them that it is better if the body is held upright so that the breathing and the flow of energy is unhindered.

To demonstrate this to them, ask the children to slump over so that the body is bent forward. Ask them to notice their breathing, then to experience the difference in how breathing feels when they are sitting up straight (without straining). If the children are sitting on chairs, it is better if their feet can comfortably reach the floor. Again, they should sit with their backs straight but relaxed, their arms and hands relaxed, their heads straight, and their necks relaxed. When they are ready, they should close their eyes. If some of them find this difficult, encourage them to focus their eyes on one thing, for example, a mark or a pattern on the floor or carpet in front of them. Their eyes should be lowered, and looking only about two metres away.

Breathing

Watching the breath
Sitting correctly and quietly in the circle, begin meditating by focusing on the breath (Chapter 4). For five-years-olds this can be harder than you might anticipate. For older children, it comes more easily. But even with the little ones, a tried-and-tested method is to ask them to be aware of the air, cool as it enters the nose and warmer as they breathe out. The first time they do this you will probably find that their breathing becomes very exaggerated. Many of the children will breathe in with all their might, almost pink with effort and somewhat noisily; breathing out will be similarly spectacular with huge and grateful releases of breath. Gently remind them that they should breath normally. It helps if you demonstrate this by asking them to watch you as you talk them through it:

> Watch as I breathe in normally. [Demonstrate this.] I can feel the cool air as it enters my nose. [For the youngest children, point to your nose.] Now I am breathing out normally [breathe out normally, still pointing to your nose], and I can feel the warm air as it comes out through my nose. Now I'll show you the whole thing without speaking. [Just breathe in and out normally.] Now see if you can do that.

This usually works first time, although there may be one or two who rather enjoy exaggerating, but who soon settle down to join the others. Ask them to do this for about five breaths and then stop. Gentle encouragement and practice will soon allow them to do this naturally.

To begin with they will be able to maintain this for about

three complete breaths (i.e. in and out) at the most. This exercise encourages concentration, focus and awareness. It also helps the children to become more aware of their breathing which in turn can enhance their health. A case study in the following chapter (p. 154) illustrates this.

Now suggest that they sit really quietly with their eyes closed, while you count up to five under your breath. Count up to five under your breath, then say, 'When you are ready, you can open your eyes.' These are the first steps to a 'sitting' meditation. If there is time, you may want a few children to talk about how it felt. If not, ensure that your voice remains soft as you direct them to their next activity.

Counting the breath
Here the children are encouraged to breathe in slowly to the count of three, hold the breath for the count of three, and then breathe out to the count of three. This is a good exercise for breath control, concentration and self-awareness. Children may not at first take easily to this exercise so, as with everything, we need to add interest. You can do this by asking the children to take it in turns to do the counting for the others. This involves three children at a time. The first counts 'in, two, three', the second 'hold, two, three' and the third 'out, two, three'. This actually requires some practice since some younger children become flustered and excited when it is their turn to count, and tend to forget which is their line or suddenly become too shy to say it. Gentle perseverance is needed. They will be able to do it with practice. Because they enjoy doing this so much, you must ensure that everyone has a turn. It is important that the counting should be rhythmical, not too fast and not too slow, and this is no mean feat in itself. You need, of course, to demonstrate the whole set of instructions very evenly and rhythmically yourself, so that the children are able to hear what they are aiming for. Three complete rounds of in, hold and out is usually enough at first. With a group of nine children, this will allow each child to have a turn at both the

breathing and the counting, and is in itself a study in concentration and self-control.

Either or both of the following visualization exercises follow on well after the breathing exercises.

The exercises

Visualization and drawing
As we stressed in Chapter 9, visualization encourages concentration, creativity and self-knowledge. For the following exercise, you need to provide the children with sheets of paper, pens and crayons. Children can draw quite well while resting their paper on the floor, unless it is carpeted, in which case they will need something firm upon which to lean. Make sure that they write their name and the date on their paper, as this allows you to look at the changes in their drawings over time.

The children should remain in their relaxed but upright sitting position with their eyes closed. Speak to them softly, as follows.

> Keep your eyes closed and imagine a place inside your head, just above the top of your nose and between your eyes. Imagine there is a white screen there, now allow yourself to see any pictures on the screen that come into your mind.

After about thirty to forty seconds, ask them to stop. Each child should have a chance to talk about, as well as draw a picture of, what they saw. Although praise is an important part of teaching and indeed of any interactions with children, it must be stressed that during any activities when children report their feelings or experiences, *you should not praise the content of their experiences* as this will inevitably serve to shape their future responses. They might well end up producing what they think you want to hear or see. Just be interested and listen, maybe asking a little more about their experiences if you feel it would be helpful to them. Experience of this activity has shown that over only a few weeks the content of their reported pictures changes considerably. Boys often first report seeing Action Man or scenes from adventure films or other stereotypical male responses, while girls see their friends skipping or their dolls, again fairly stereotypical female responses. After a few sessions children sometimes start reporting things like 'I saw my granny who died a long time ago and she smiled at me' or 'my aunty who died came to visit us and it was nice' or sometimes they report encountering living relatives whom they see only occasionally. This seems to be a source of comfort or pleasure to children. Later still, they begin to say other more imaginative things; one little boy said, 'I saw elephants washing themselves', another said, 'I saw hippopotamuses playing in the mud' and a little girl said, 'I saw myself on a white bird flying in the sky'. Without passing value judgements on these experiences, it does seem that they show an interesting and positive development.

The Wheel
Ask the group to lie down on the floor in their circle with their feet pointing inwards, like a wheel. You should remain sitting outside the circle as at this point you may find yourself needing to encourage the children not to play around with other people's feet by sliding their own across and pushing them. Often when children do something they have never done before, particularly when it increases their self-consciousness, they cover their embarrassment by joking or disrupting someone else, thus directing attention away from themselves or the activity. This is natural, and as they get used to the activity you will find this problem becomes less as self-awareness and self-confidence develop and generalize to other situations. Once the children are in position, talk to them in a gentle voice and ask them to relax. It is better if they are on their backs but some may feel too vulnerable and prefer to turn onto their sides. That is all right; it may change

later as they see the others on their backs and realize that is safe. Again, this is a moment for giggles and little points of physical contact. Gentle persuasion will usually be enough to stop this.

Ask the children to be aware of their body, to feel the floor beneath them, to relax their feet and then their legs, and follow this relaxation all the way up to their backs, arms, shoulders and neck, and finally their face. (More details of this kind of activity are to be found in Chapter 7.) Ask them to imagine that they all make up a wheel, which is moving slowly round to the left. Wave your arms to the left as some of them may not know left from right. After about fifteen seconds, ask them to imagine the wheel going the other way, still with their eyes closed. After a further fifteen seconds, stop. This has allowed them to feel a connection with each other as all of them have formed an essential part of the wheel.

Continue the activity by asking them to imagine themselves in a favourite place – maybe in their bedroom, in the garden, beside a stream or on the beach. While their eyes are closed, speak the following words gently and slowly to them. Make sure that you pause long enough after each suggestion for them to experience the different sensations.

> Stay lying down. Keeping your eyes closed, use your mind to look around and see all the things around you. Maybe you can also hear sounds. Perhaps you can touch things; notice what they feel like. You are lying in your favourite place feeling very happy and peaceful. Now you can see your favourite person or pet coming along to join you. He or she sits down next to you; maybe you talk to one another. Listen to what you say to each other, think about how you feel. Now your friend or animal has to leave and you say goodbye. You are on your own again, still feeling peaceful, knowing that you will meet your friend again. [Pause.] You are now back in the room, in school, with your friends around you. When you are ready, open your eyes and sit up.

It is important to give each child a chance to share his or her experience with the group. You will usually find that this is a pleasant experience for all of them, so you can tell them that they can go back to this special place whenever they wish.

Music

Another activity which is conducive to meditation is music. We have already mentioned the value of playing music softly as the children enter the meditation room, but they can also make their own. If you have some percussion instruments, so much the better; if not, then inventiveness with plastic washing-up liquid bottles decorated and filled with dried peas or lentils etc. can be an effective substitute. If you have percussion instruments, it is better to begin by using only the relatively quiet ones. As the children's self-control and concentration increases, all the instruments may be used. Young children love playing with percussion instruments, and will probably want to have a turn on more than one of them. They also like to push the instruments to their limits, that is to play them as loudly as they can and generally experiment with them. Initially you can be forgiven for the use of bribery. For example, you might say to them that if they are very good and show that they can play well, you will let them play what they like at the end of the whole session. This generally does the trick until they learn to enjoy control, and begin to play naturally in a concentrated and creative way. Let them experiment gently, then choose a peaceful song, perhaps a lullaby, to sing. Encourage the children to watch carefully as you point to the instruments to indicate when each is to play and when to stop. This increases their concentration, co-ordination and co-operative team skills. Do this several times. When you feel they are ready, repeat the song and encourage the children to listen carefully and decide for themselves how to accompany it. Finally, as you promised, let the children change their instruments if they wish, and allow them free expression for one or two minutes.

Ensure that they put the instruments back where they came from, before returning to the circle.

As the children become more centred and calm through meditation and related activities, they will each be able to play their instrument softly and harmoniously without direction from the teacher, by listening very carefully to all the other children's instruments. This can be quite an intense form of joyful meditation.

Keeping the instruments until the end of the session can be helpful as an incentive to the children to behave for the rest of the lesson. If they think that there is the remotest possibility that they may be deprived of this pleasure, they can usually demonstrate quite exemplary behaviour throughout.

Closing the session
It is always a good thing to end the session by sitting in the circle together, doing the basic breathing exercise three times and then continuing to sit in silence for a further twenty seconds, building up to a minute over several sessions. This is much harder for some children than one might anticipate, so initially the strategy of saying, 'let's see who can sit really quietly while I count up to twenty under my breath', generally has an amazing effect. Gradually you can increase the time to one minute, and soon the children will be able to sit without inducement. Some children, even as young as five years old, take to this naturally, and can sit for relatively long periods undisturbed by anything going on around them. Not surprisingly, these children also tend to find all the other activities relatively easy. But even the very lively ones can eventually participate in all of them.

The session should end with the children leaving the circle and quietly putting on their shoes. If they don't have far to go to their class, they can leave when they are ready. If they have to wait for you to take them back, they should line up and return to their class in a quiet and orderly fashion. Teachers have often reported their surprise at how changed, quiet and focused the children are for some considerable time after they return from the session. The following comment is not unusual after a meditation session. 'I couldn't believe it, they came back quietly, just got on with their work and were wonderful all day. They worked hard and even the livelier ones didn't get into any trouble.'

Opting out

After you have given all the children an opportunity to experience a few sessions, if some of them really do not wish to continue, it is better to let them opt out. They may just not be ready, but the seeds will have been sown, and they may change their minds later, and start again from the beginning with a new group.

MEDITATION WITH THE WHOLE CLASS

As mentioned above, this is a good way for all the children to experience some meditation and the related activities. We now need to go further and provide recommendations for how meditation can best be incorporated into work with the whole class. It can be used regularly at particular times of the day as a settling down and focusing activity, and at times it may be extended to include visualization and drawing as well as communication and listening. If your class also undertakes the group meditation described above, so much the better. The length of the whole class meditation session will depend on both the constraints within your timetable and on the way the children respond at any given time. But another benefit is that not only does the meditation session help to centre the children, it can serve to centre you and help you to feel more relaxed.

Regular short meditations

As mentioned earlier, a short session is a very good way to start the day. Probably your present practice for beginning the day is to have everyone sitting quietly while you take the register. It is right that this should come first, as the latecomers can fit in easily without missing anything from another session. So a good place for the first meditation of the day is after the register. Often register is followed by an assembly, but you can usually still fit in a few moments meditation before this happens. Your usual practice when taking the register may be to have all the children sitting around you, or you may prefer them to sit on chairs at their tables. If they are at tables, ask them to turn their chairs so that they are all facing you. Using the floor is another option; all the children need do is spread out so they are not touching each other. Make sure that they have nothing in their hands.

Talking about meditation

Before you begin the actual exercises, you should talk to the children about meditation or, if you do not wish to use the term 'meditation', the exercises you are about to teach them. It is important to tell the children why you are teaching them meditation. Children like to see a point to an activity, especially when they have nothing immediately concrete to show for it. Explain to them that it will help them with their work and it will help them get on better with their friends. (See Chapter 1 for more benefits.) Allow them to ask questions, as all children love to do, and if you have read the rest of this book you will be able to field comfortably any questions the children might ask. Here are some questions that come up and some suggestions for possible answers.

Q.   How will meditation help us with our work?

A.   Sometimes when you are working and other

children are being noisy or doing something you would prefer to be doing, it is hard for you to concentrate. Perhaps you leave what you are doing and join in, then get into trouble. Or perhaps you just get fed up and then you don't want to finish what you are doing. Then you don't do your best work. Practising meditation helps you not to be put off so easily, and it helps you to feel more settled.

Q.   How will it help us get on better with our friends?

A.   It can help you to be more thoughtful and to think before you do something that will upset someone else. It may help you not to get angry and to be more considerate, and then people will like you more and there will not be so much to quarrel about.

Although it will not be necessary to invite questions before every meditation session, it is a good idea to request them from time to time to remind the children, and yourself, of the benefits of meditation.

This is a good time to talk to the children about the importance of respecting other people's space and wishes, so that seductive activities such as prodding or pulling hair become considered to be unsociable and inconsiderate things to do. A short discussion about considerate behaviour in general could be introduced by asking the children to think of ways in which they like to be treated. Ask them to think of behaviours which they consider to be kind and thoughtful and behaviours which they dislike. Maybe they can think of someone they particularly like or admire and discuss what they particularly like about them. This will lead naturally to the idea that we should treat others as we would like them to treat us, and will heighten the children's awareness and help them to realize the effect they have upon other people. If this is practised often, it should eventually have a long-term effect, in encouraging more controlled and thoughtful behaviour until it becomes natural.

Sitting correctly

With their awareness of consideration for others heightened, let the children shuffle into a comfortable position, with hands on laps and fingers relaxed. They should sit with straight backs, without straining. They should feel comfortable and relaxed. There is no special position for the hands, but you will probably find that some will place them into a traditional Buddhist position, perhaps because they have seen it in pictures or on television. Others will copy whatever they see you do, as they will think this is right. Others will find their own way. At this stage, it really doesn't matter as long as they are relaxed and focused. If they are on the floor, then sitting cross-legged is probably easiest for them. If they are on chairs, it is better if their legs are side by side with both their feet touching the floor.

They may do the following exercise with their eyes open if they wish, as some children initially feel vulnerable closing their eyes in the course of the day with other people around them. It is important to remember that meditation is an activity unlike anything they will have done before. Saying prayers is probably the closest thing to it they will have experienced, but in prayer they repeat words whereas you will be asking them to do nothing. You will probably find that most children will close their eyes straight away, and after a few sessions the rest will probably close them quite naturally too.

If there are any children who do not want to join in, they should sit quietly and either just watch or look at a book. They should be discouraged from getting up and walking about as this is disruptive, at least in the early learning stages of meditation.

Breathing

Watching the breath

This is described in detail in the previous section for meditation with small groups and will last for only thirty seconds to one minute. The children should sit correctly, eyes usually closed, not touching anyone else, hands empty, feet on the ground if they are on chairs, all facing you. If they are on the floor, sit down with them. If they are on chairs, sit on a chair too. Ask the children to become aware of their breath, as described in Chapter 4.

This short meditation may be repeated as many times as you like. It is a good and constructive way to calm a noisy class or to mark the change over of sessions. At the very least, it makes a good way to start and end the morning, and to start and end the afternoon. After a while, it will come so naturally that the children will really miss it should you forget.

Remember that even in the midst of a hectic and busy school environment these quiet meditative breaks can also help to calm and centre *you*; and the more centred you are, the more centred will be the children. To quote one teacher after a meditation session with six- to seven-year-olds, 'That was lovely. I feel quite calm and relaxed. It's really made a difference to my day.'

Counting the breath

After several sessions of short meditation, go on to the next step, which adds only another thirty seconds to one minute. This is the counting and breathing exercise outlined in the group exercises on page 132. This exercise can be easily adapted to the whole class situation. Make sure that all the children have their turn at being responsible for counting aloud over a period of days. Once they have all had a turn, you can do the counting yourself, up to a maximum of five complete breaths, one breath being 'In, two, three . . . hold, two, three . . . out, two, three'.

Longer meditations

Begin with the usual short meditation (watching the breath), followed by the breathing exercise (counting the breath). Introduce some visualization and let the children subsequently describe or draw what they see. The ideas earlier in this chapter can easily be adapted for a whole class activity. Further exercises which might be appropriate here, such as the drawing of an everyday object from memory, are outlined in Chapter 3.

MEDITATION AT HOME

Introducing home meditation

Introduce home meditation as something which will help the children in their work at school and as something that may be fun. You can also explain that it may help them with their friendships, and with everything that they do. The discussion in the previous section on whole class meditation will provide more ideas for introducing the topic. You will also need to demonstrate that you meditate for the same reasons yourself, and, of course, you will need to do the exercises alongside your children.

One of the big virtues of this session for the children is that not only do they gain from the meditative experience itself but they also receive your undivided attention, and this in itself serves to enhance your relationship further as you share pleasant, equitable and relaxing times together.

The time

With children as young as five to seven years old, the home meditation sessions and related activities will probably take between five and ten minutes. A good time for meditation at home is shortly before bedtime. If children think that meditation will give them that extra few minutes of staying up it will probably gain instant favour. Meditating at bedtime will also mean that meditation is not competing with playing with friends or with their favourite television programmes and they won't be in a hurry to finish because of something they are planning to do immediately afterwards.

The setting

You will need a fairly quiet room where you are not easily distracted, maybe your child or children's bedroom, if there is enough space. The room should not be too brightly lit but not dingy either; a soft side light is often just the right thing. You will need to ask the rest of the family, if they don't want to join in, to be a little quieter just for that short period. You might even have a friendly notice on the door of the room you use, saying 'meditation in progress, please don't disturb' or some such thing, so that other family members respect your time and space for the period concerned.

It is better if you and the children are in loose clothing, with feet either bare or just in socks. Everyone should feel free and relaxed. It is nice to have special clothing for the session, such as lightweight tracksuits or special pyjamas, something you all really like wearing, and which helps to create the right frame of mind.

The exercises

Movement

Before the first meditation session, do a few gentle stretching and relaxing movements together, such as stretching wide and relaxing, then stretching high and relaxing. There are several possible subsequent approaches to the first session, and if you have read the rest of this book you may already have several ideas of your own. Here is one suggestion suitable for a lively child.

Sitting quietly

Sit on the floor opposite one another and say to your child, 'Let's play some games together'. He or she will probably imagine that you are going to play something lively and boisterous, so you will need to point out that these games are new and different from others that you may have played together.

Begin by saying, 'First, let's see if we can both sit really still while I count up to five.' The number to which you choose to count will depend on what you think your child can comfortably achieve. It is important that you do not ask your child to do something of which he or she is incapable. This can only end in frustration and disappointment for both of you. You can always move to a slightly higher target as the activity becomes easier. We cannot emphasize enough that in any activity with your child you should *always choose a target that is within his or her reach*. It doesn't always need to be within easy reach as effort is necessary for progress, but it must be possible.

Sit really quietly together as you count to five. Remember to praise any effort your child or children have made. Ask them to close their eyes. If they are reluctant to do so, you might help it along by suggesting a 'copy me game': 'I'll sit quietly and shut my eyes while you count up to five, then you sit quietly and shut your eyes while I count up to five.' The fact that you are taking it in turns should help the children to feel more comfortable and should make the whole activity more of a game and more equitable. Already, albeit for only five seconds, the children are consciously taking control of themselves and experiencing quiet moments.

The following activities can be difficult for children as young as three or four years old. It is up to you to choose the activities which you feel are most suited to your children. Often trial and error will help you to discover this.

Watching the breath and counting the breath
Detailed instructions for these breathing exercises with young school children were given earlier on page 132. Watching the breath simply requires us to focus on the cool air entering the nose as we breathe in and the warmer air leaving as we exhale. Counting the breath requires more breath control as we breath in, hold our breath, then exhale, each to the count of three.

Music
You might follow the breathing exercises by using percussion instruments. Ideally you should have one instrument of the same kind each, so that again you can play the 'copy me' game. Play a short rhythm, a maximum of three or four beats to start with, and ask the children to copy you. Do this a few times, then ask each in turn to do the same while you copy.

Visualization and drawing
This activity should immediately follow the breathing exercises. You will need to have some paper, pencils and crayons for this session. Ask your child or children to keep their eyes closed, and imagine a white screen above the nose and between the eyes. Ask if they can see any pictures on the screen. Encourage them either to talk to you about what they have seen and/or to draw pictures of the images.

Rosie
Rosie was six years old. Her parents were going through a particularly difficult period in their marriage and, although both parents remained as loving and caring as ever to her, Rosie felt torn in her loyalties to them. She sometimes experienced considerable ambivalence and anger towards them. Rosie found the breathing exercises easy and enjoyed the 'tunnel and light' visualization (pp. 162–3). When talking about her experience of the visualization afterwards, she reported that the people in the light had been the people

she loved most in the world. She had seen her 'mummy, daddy and sister' all smiling at her. It had felt lovely and seemed to help to put things back into perspective again.

Rosie also reported that it had been hard to visualize the white screen first and this is something on which children vary considerably.

You might also draw a picture of something you might have visualized yourself. When you have all finished, spend a minute or two talking about the pictures. You must be careful about the way you praise the children's efforts. As we said earlier, praise the effort but not the content of the pictures because content praise often serves to bias the content of future pictures. If the children think, for example, that you consider their drawing of a house is exciting and wonderful, they might keep on producing houses to please you. If, despite your care to be non-judgemental about their drawings, they draw the same thing every time, resist the temptation to say, 'that's very nice, but you did that last time, try to think of something else'. Such a remark suggests that either you are bored with seeing them draw houses, and would like variety, or that you think it is important for them to draw something else. If they draw what they see, then they have done what you have asked of them. The fact might be that the children like or need to draw dolls or houses or aeroplanes many times for a reason which might not be immediately obvious. Encourage them to talk to you about their productions.

The older the children, the longer you can spend on these activities. But much will depend on individual children. Remember to offer them achievable goals, and always praise them for their efforts. If they get fed up after a short while, and gentle encouragement has no effect, then conclude the activity and introduce it at another time. Never force a session to go on, and remember that gentle persistence is often the most effective way to achieve things with children.

Larger family group

It is relatively easy to adapt the above activities to a larger family group by making sure that you all take things in turn. For example, for the music activity, each person should have the opportunity to tap out a rhythm which the others copy. But remember that the youngest family members need short, interesting activities with plenty of variety. It might be that when the youngest has had enough, you can close the session so that he or she can go to bed. The rest of you can then carry on later at a pace and length that suits you. It is important that you have enough confidence to modify these activities until you find what suits your child or family best. As long as the exercises are carried out with love and joy you will not go far wrong.

Chapter 14

Beginning Meditation with Nine- to Twelve-Year-Olds

With the younger group in the previous chapter, length of concentration was one of the main factors which needed to be taken into account. Although the children in this section are older, and one would expect them to find meditation and related activities easier, there are different constraining factors now in play. Generally older children are less easily cajoled into activities which do not have instant appeal, are often very self-conscious as well as image-conscious and often need to see a convincing reason for doing anything new and different, especially if their friends are not involved in the activity.

INTRODUCING THE TOPIC

Talking to older children about the benefits of meditation and what it can do for them will help. You do not even have to refer to it as meditation, but as exercises and techniques which will enable the children to be more in control of their own minds and bodies. One obvious appeal to the sports-inclined children (as we pointed out in Chapter 1) will be that it can improve concentration, focus and mind-body co-ordination, thereby improving their overall performance. Academically inclined children will be interested to learn that increased concentration can bring them equal benefits (Chapter 4), while creative children will respond to the knowledge that meditation can enhance fluency and flexibility of thought (Chapter 8). Of course, none of these attributes are necessarily mutually exclusive. For all children, an added advantage is that the exercises can also improve social skills, allowing them to relate better to other children, gaining more poise and self-confidence, which in turn can make them more attractive people. As you explain these things, even those children who appear disinterested or dismissive are likely at some level to be listening and taking it in.

If the more popular children in the class are seen to approve of meditation and related activities, it increases the chance that many of the others will follow suit, as the 'stars' are often taken as role models by the others. It does no harm, therefore, to make a subtle effort to appeal to these children. One dilemma when working with older age groups is how to present the concept of meditation. To some, the use of terms such as 'meditation' or 'spirituality' will be alienating, either because they will perceive them as 'airy fairy nonsense' or because they feel embarrassed at the thought of being involved in anything so strange. Others, however, will welcome the whole idea of spirituality, meditation and other esoteric activities. Such undertakings will stir up feelings of excitement at the thought of the 'unknown' and the 'mystical' or will engender feelings of longing for their own spiritual development. We have no simple answer for getting around these conflicting responses. Your own intuition and knowledge of the children you are going to work with must guide you. You may decide to refer to meditation as exercises for developing physical and mental potential, or you may prefer to create two separate sessions, each with a different name and emphasis, so that the children can choose which they prefer. For example, one session might be called 'Exercises and Techniques for Increasing Your Life Control', and the other 'Meditation for Creativity and Spirituality'. Although you would cover very similar ground with the two groups, you would present it in different ways, with a change of emphasis on the various activities as appropriate. You would also be aware of the different moods and needs of each group, together with their preferred levels of activity, their attention span and their liking for variety.

MEDITATION WITH SMALL GROUPS

Preparing the room

When working with small groups of fifteen or less, many of the same conditions described in Chapter 13 for the younger children will apply. It is helpful to work always in the same room, with as few distractions as possible. The children should get into the habit of taking their shoes off on entering the room, and lining them up neatly. Take yours off as well. The room should be set up ready for them. If they are to sit on chairs, then these should be placed in a circle, so that the children can immediately seat themselves without having to shift things around. If they are to sit on a hard floor, they should either bring cushions with them and seat themselves quietly, or cushions should be laid out in advance for them in a circle. If there is a carpet, they may sit directly on the floor, and should do so as soon as they have taken off their shoes. As with the younger children, you should take your place in the circle as soon as convenient, and before the children if possible so that they can come and join you. This has an immediate calming effect on them. Soft music playing as they enter and during the session (soothing 'New Age' is good for this) can help to create a tranquil atmosphere, especially if accompanied by a burning incense stick, although the latter may not always be practical.

Consideration for others

At the beginning of the first session, you need to lay down some ground rules of acceptable behaviour. This should be done sensitively and firmly, but not dogmatically. Point out to the children the importance of respecting other people's wishes and explain that people appreciate being allowed to carry out an activity without interruption. Allow a few minutes for discussion of this. You might begin by asking the children what characteristics they like in others, and how they themselves like to be treated. Developing consideration for others and becoming aware of its positive effects for everyone, including themselves, will always stand them in good stead.

Confidentiality

Make a group agreement that everything shared in this session is confidential to the group. Also, assure the children that they do not have to share any of their experiences with the group if they choose not to. The thought that they may have to make public their experiences may inhibit the way in which they approach the exercise.

Beginning the session

Relaxation

Begin each session with a short relaxation exercise. But first explain the advantages of relaxation and of body awareness, reminding them of the inextricable connection between body and mind, especially the power of the mind over the body, and our responsibility to look after them both. You might even quote some basic research describing how some people whose doctors had given up hope of a recovery got better, due to their positive attitude, while others who allowed themselves to despair remained ill. For a fuller discussion on this see Chapter 1.

Make sure that the children are sitting in a relaxed position, usually either cross-legged on the floor or on upright chairs. Their backs should be straight but not stiff, and their heads upright, tilted neither upwards nor downwards. You might wish to tell them that the reason for this is to allow their energy to travel freely throughout their bodies. You will need to check them swiftly and gently and suggest any needed adjustments. The children can be told that it is easier if they close their eyes, but should they find this difficult they can choose a spot about two metres in front of them and gaze at it with their eyes lowered. Talk them unhurriedly through the relaxation, asking them to pay attention to their body, making sure that they are relaxed from their feet, toes and legs upwards to their shoulders, neck, face etc., so that they are aware that their whole body feels relaxed. Allow enough time for them to focus on each of the body parts as you proceed.

Watching the breath and counting the breath
Introduce the techniques for watching the breath and counting the breath as explained on pages 131–2. Tell them that if they find thoughts entering their head (which they almost certainly will), this is quite natural and they should let them go, allowing them to float away. Emphasize that no great effort should be used; the thoughts should gently be released. They may find the use of imagery helpful, for example imagining that their thoughts float away on a cloud or in a balloon. The time spent on this will vary according to the age and concentration of the children, but a rough guide to start with would be about thirty seconds for the nine-year-olds, moving up to one minute for the eleven-year-olds. These times can be gradually increased with practice.

After practice, the children will be able to do these breathing exercises on their own, that is, without you counting for them, but remind them from time to time gently to let go of any thoughts. These two exercises, watching the breath and counting the breath, will together take about three minutes. Below is a case study which shows how these breathing exercises helped a young asthmatic boy to overcome his breathing problems.

Paul

Brenda, a parent who has discussed her experiences with us, recounted how these breathing exercises helped her asthmatic son, Paul, who was then nine years old. After several sessions of the breathing exercises, Paul needed to use his inhaler less and less and two years later had dispensed with it altogether. His mother originally broached the subject of these exercises by telling Paul that they would help him with his breathing, and that they would enable him to do his school work more quickly by aiding his powers of focus and concentration. She spoke to him about the relationship between the mind and the body and explained that he had a responsibility to look after his body to the best of his ability. Paul particularly liked the idea of the control over his own body which these exercises would bring. Paul was keen on sport, and decided that this control would enhance his performance. He had also been bothered about using his inhaler in front of his friends since he perceived it as indicating weakness.

After the initial breathing exercise, 'watching the breath', while allowing distracting thoughts gently to disperse, Paul's mother found that asking him to focus on an object while continuing with the exercise was particularly helpful. She chose an orange, which Paul looked at carefully as they sat silently together. Afterwards they would talk about the experience, and Paul would tell Brenda what he had seen in the orange, and what he had experienced. Brenda also told us that today Paul still does not accept the idea of meditation or anything vaguely out of the ordinary, but now at seventeen he still has no need of an inhaler, and continues to meditate (although he would not term it that), particularly in times of stress or fear, such as during preparations for exams.

Paul's story provides us with further useful insights. He would not have agreed to do the exercises if they had initially been framed as meditation or as anything vaguely esoteric, and at seventeen years old he still holds the same opinion. The way in which you present the activities to your children is therefore most important. We are not suggesting that if one of your children has asthma, you should abandon medication in favour of the breathing exercises. Nevertheless, the child may, like Paul, find that, with medical approval, the inhaler is needed less and less. Similarly, no claims of any kind should be made that meditation will help children with any specific physical problems. However, it can be of value with things such as breathing and concentration, and it can help to reduce stress and that in turn can have a beneficial effect on one's health.

You may like to try with your children an extended version of Paul's concentration exercise involving an orange. You will need to provide either one orange per child, or per pair of children, or per group. In the latter case, you should place the orange in the middle of the group so that everyone has a clear view of it. This should follow the basic meditation breathing technique of watching and counting the breath. Encourage the children to sit quietly ready for the visualization exercise.

The exercises

Visualization for concentration and focus
Ask the children to look at their orange which should be placed in front of them. Tell them that they are going to experience everything there is to experience about an orange without actually touching it. Remind them to sit in their meditation position, upright but not stiff, and then to focus upon the orange. Ask them to join you in the visualization outlined here.

> Look carefully at the orange, notice its shape. Is it completely round? Is it oval? How would *you* describe its shape? Now look at its colour – is it a dark orange, a light orange, is it an even colour all over or can you see traces of different colours or shades of colour? What does the skin look like? Is it smooth? Can you see the uneven texture and the

dimples in its skin? Can you see its shininess? Holding this picture in your mind you may now choose to close your eyes and imagine the rest, or you may keep your eyes open, whichever feels more comfortable. Without moving, imagine what it would be like to touch the orange, to squeeze it gently. In your mind pick it up and feel its weight, feel its soft dimply skin. Imagine the smell of your orange. Now imagine peeling your orange. Notice the fine spray of juice which is released as you break the skin and begin to peel it away from the flesh. Look at the soft white pith, feel its softness. Gradually peel the pith away to reveal the orange segments which fit so perfectly together. Imagine what it would be like to remove a segment, feel its firm fleshiness between your fingers, smell the luscious orangy smell. Now place the segment in your mouth, feel it cool on your tongue and taste it.

Now I'm going to ask you to reverse the process, like winding back a video tape going through each stage carefully until you see the orange whole again as it sits on the table.

You might allow them to reverse the process in their own time or you might talk them through it by amending the above text as necessary. The whole exercise, including the breathing, will probably take around five minutes, but remember to give the instructions slowly enough for them to guide the imagination.

By the time children are this age it might be taken for granted that they have all experienced eating an orange, but this might not be the case. If you intend to use this exercise it would be useful to have a session beforehand in which all the children bring oranges to school (spares can be brought for those who don't bring their own) and slowly go mindfully through the process of eating them together.

You will probably find that, during the exercise and in the actual eating process, some children will not like the experience and will make faces and choking noises to amuse their friends. This is natural, and familiarity with other 'odd' exercises will soon eliminate these responses. For those who don't like oranges other fruits may be substituted and the instructions modified accordingly.

After they have experienced the 'real thing' as suggested, a version of the above exercise may be done entirely through imagination with anything – fruit, pencils, animals . . . Of course, to state the blatantly obvious, the instructions for each object will have to be tailored for that specific object. Children can imagine drawing, writing, building something or even practising a skill. The possibilities are endless.

Such exercises as these require considerable focus and concentration, and can lead children into many strange and interesting worlds of imagination. Again, both you and the children will be able to think of many more objects to use for this exercise.

Guided visualization

For this exercise you should provide paper, pens, pencils and crayons, as when the exercise is over the children may wish to draw or write about their experiences.

Without breaking the flow of the session, speak gently and slowly to the children.

> Close your eyes and imagine a door in front of you. Maybe it is a door that you recognize or maybe it is a door which you have never seen before. Look at it carefully, notice what it looks like and how you feel. Now open the door, and as you walk through it you find yourself in a place where you feel happy and safe. It may be somewhere you already know, or it may be a place that you create for yourself. Look around carefully at all the things you can see. As you walk along, look for a favourite place to settle down. Notice how you are feeling. When you have found your favourite place, sit or lie down and feel completely safe and relaxed.

Try not to give too many suggestions as you guide the children along, as the experience should come from their own imagination. Allow them a minute to relax in their favourite place, enjoying whatever sensations come to them, then gently call them back.

> When you are ready, slowly get up and begin to walk back to the door. Look at everything around you and notice how you are feeling. When you get to the door, open it if it is closed, and walk through. Think about how you are feeling now. Once you are on the other side of the door, gently close it, knowing that you can return there any time, and that your own special place of safety and comfort will always be there for you.

Assure them that they can return to this place whenever they wish, that it is their own special place. If you feel more confident reading the visualization rather doing it from memory, write down the above, expanding on it as appropriate.

When you have asked the children to do something such as looking around or noticing how they feel, it is important that you pause long enough for them to experience their reactions fully before you guide them onto the next part of the visualization.

As a follow-up to this activity, the children might wish to talk about their experiences, so schedule time for this into the programme. Alternatively they may prefer to draw a picture of their experiences, or to write about them to keep as a record for themselves. Make sure that every piece of work is dated so that it is possible to follow the progression. The session should end with everyone back in the circle and centred again before they leave quietly to return to their class.

Free visualization
This should follow on from breathing exercises as described above. When the children have finished the breathing exercises, ask them to focus on a place above the bridge of the nose and between the eyes. Ask them to let go of thoughts as they did during the breathing exercises, and to notice any images which may appear on this internal screen. For this exercise, allow them as long as feels comfortable, then gently bring them back into the room. Again, allow the children time to talk about their experiences and to draw or write about the images if they wish. They may choose to share their pictures and writing with others, or to keep them to themselves.

MEDITATION WITH THE WHOLE CLASS

Timing

As with younger children, it is ideal to practise with this age group the basic meditation technique of watching the breath several times a day. It takes only one or two minutes, and its beneficial effect can permeate all other activities, both for you and for the children, particularly if you meditate with the children and thus reap the direct benefits yourself. As with younger children, the most effective times for meditation are first thing after register in the morning, immediately before the lunch break, first thing after the afternoon register, and finally last thing in the afternoon. You might also spend a minute or two before and after morning break or whenever the class seems to become restless. Just stop the session, ask the children to sit down, relax their body, and talk them through the first breathing exercise.

As we explained in our earlier chapters, there is a range of activities which are related to and support meditative techniques, and these can be integrated into some of the children's timetabled work. We can now look at some of the practicalities involved.

Introducing meditation into timetabled work

Art lessons

An art lesson should begin with a short meditation, followed by one of the visualizations above or one chosen from those described in Chapter 9, e.g. the visualization of abstract shapes. The children can then be allowed to choose from a variety of different media to create an interpretation of their visualization. Some may wish to construct a three-dimensional image, while others may choose to create collages, or to paint or draw. These creations will be particularly personal to the children and praise should be given for the effort that has gone into them, and for the children's use of materials, and not for the content. As with younger children, praise of content may result in the children producing things to please, rather than allowing their experiences free rein. If children are reluctant to produce anything from their meditation, then allow them that choice. It is important at the early stages of meditation not to force things or associate the exercises with negative experiences. Other art lessons can make use of the exercises described in Chapter 3, such as drawing things from unusual angles, or drawing the spaces between objects rather than the objects themselves.

If the children are drawing spaces between displayed objects, it is initially helpful to place the objects in front of a plain, preferably contrasting, background with a frame around them. For example, you could use a black sheet of paper, with a square chalked upon it in white, large enough to frame the objects comfortably. Begin with only two objects, otherwise it could be confusing for the children.

The training in concentration and observation derived from such activities will quickly become apparent to the children.

PE or movement classes
The body awareness exercises described in Chapter 7 can
readily be incorporated into a PE or movement lesson. Begin
by asking the children to walk around the room slowly,
preferably with their eyes lowered, making sure that they do
not touch anyone else. Next, instruct them as follows.

> Now while you are walking about, I'd like you to
> think about your body. Concentrate very hard and
> see if you can work out which parts of your body
> are involved in walking. Which parts of your
> body can you feel moving as you walk? What do
> they feel like?

You can pause here while the children tell you what they
have discovered. Allow a few minutes for this, then guide
them through the observation of some of the more obvious
parts of the body used in walking. (For example, 'Walk very
very slowly, as in films shown in slow motion.') Be prepared
for some of them to try this out with stylized exaggerated
walking, but they should soon settle down.

> Notice which part of your foot touches the floor
> first, and then see what happens. Be aware of your
> feet. Feel your heel touching the floor, how your foot
> rocks forward, and the feeling as your weight is
> transferred to the ball of your foot and then to your
> toes. Notice how your knee feels as it flexes and
> straightens, how it feels when your weight is on it,
> and how it feels when you lift it up again. Feel the
> movement of your hips, arms and shoulders . . .

As they become more adept at this, the children might focus
on the more subtle movements of other parts of the body,
right down to changes in their breathing. You can vary the
speed at which the children walk, increasing it to a slow run.
You can also analyze other body movements, such as
hopping, skipping or simply walking with different length

steps, from tiny to as large as they can comfortably achieve.

Now and again, apparatus such as balls or beanbags may be used. Ask the children to work in pairs standing about six paces apart, and explain that they should concentrate on throwing the ball or beanbag as accurately as possible. They should first look carefully at its destination, then be aware of the feeling as it leaves their hands, and then watch it as it travels through the air, noticing the way it moves and finally lands into the hands of their partner. You will doubtlessly be able to think of a lot more ways in which you can develop this kind of awareness before proceeding to the more specific exercises we give in Chapter 7. These preliminary exercises encourage a more concentrated awareness and meditative approach to all physical movement and may be seen as a necessary part of body education rather than as something esoteric added on to normal school work. If practised often enough, this awareness of physical movement and the ability to focus will become a natural and valuable asset to any physical activity.

Creative writing

Children can be given the opportunity to develop in prose, poetry or even dialogue the experiences resulting from their visualizations. An appropriate visualization with which to start is given below, but remember that every visualization is best preceded by the relaxation and breathing exercises already described.

After the breathing exercises, ask the children to remain still with their eyes closed. Speaking softly and slowly, allowing them enough time to experience the different sensations, talk them through the visualization. Begin by asking them to imagine a doorway.

> Look at the door carefully and, knowing that it will
> be safe to do so, open it. Upon stepping through the
> doorway, you find yourself in a tunnel. At the end
> of the tunnel you can see a bright light. Look

> around you. How do you feel? It is quite safe but you can turn back whenever you wish. Be aware of the tunnel itself – what does it looks like? As you reach the end of the tunnel, you find yourself enveloped in a bright light, and see people in front of you. As you stand facing them, you feel very warm and safe and loved. Now one of the people walks towards you, smiling. You look at each other intently, and one of you speaks. Maybe you ask a question, or maybe it is the other person who speaks first. Or you may communicate with each other telepathically, with your minds.

Allow the children a minute or two to carry on with this visualization on their own, making sure that you are giving them enough time to explore each part.

> The person then smiles, and begins to leave, moving backwards away from you. Now you move back down the tunnel, knowing that you can return whenever you like, and knowing that the person you have just met will always be there for you. Now open the door if it is closed, and walk through to the other side. Look at the door again, noticing how you feel. Now you are here in this room with all your friends. You feel safe and relaxed.

If the children are going to write about this experience, then they should do so straight away. They could write about it in prose or in poetry. They might like to write down the dialogue they had, or would like to have had, or they might speculate on how the conversation might have progressed if it had been allowed to continue. A short play might even emerge from this encounter. This could then be performed by the children themselves.

Sometimes the children might simply wish to talk about this experience or to repeat the dialogue, and time could also be made for this.

Another activity which would encourage observation, concentration and imagination could be as follows. Gather a number of interesting and not too familiar objects together, keeping them out of sight of the children. After the relaxation and breathing exercises, ask the children to close their eyes. Give each child one of these objects, telling them that any peeping will spoil the exercise. Give them a minute or two to hold the object, and explore it using whatever senses feel appropriate. While their eyes are still closed, collect in the objects and again put them out of sight. Without having seen the objects, encourage the children to write about the experience in any way they choose.

These are only a few suggestions for creative writing exercises. Once you become aware of the kinds of things that work, you will be able to add to them. Encourage the children to think of some activities of their own.

Music
Only teachers who are themselves musical may feel immediately comfortable with the use of music in meditation. However, you do not need to play an instrument to use musical exercises effectively, though it is helpful if you have a reasonable sense of rhythm, and some understanding and appreciation of sound.

Introductory meditation exercises using music can take the form of careful listening or mindful playing of an instrument. There are a number of ways in which listening and paying attention to different aspects of a musical piece can aid children's concentration and focus. One of the simplest exercises, familiar to most teachers, is to sing or play a rhythmical phrase and ask the children to copy it. This exercise, as with all of the exercises, may be increased in length and complexity according to the children's capability, discipline and interest.

Another activity involving careful listening requires playing a recording of a piece of instrumental music (lyrics are something of a distraction) and asking the children to follow one of the instruments all the way through. Either classical or popular music will do, and preferably children should be exposed to both. Initially, a piece where one or two instruments stand out more than the rest is preferable. Ask the children to focus on one of the instruments, and try to follow its melody through the piece. With practice, the pieces can become longer and more complex. This activity also helps develop appreciation of music and its complexities in a relaxed and enjoyable way.

Playing instruments can also help develop children's concentration, co-ordination, sensitivity, creativity and co-operation. Percussion instruments are generally preferable for this exercise, as they do not demand a great deal of expertise in order to play well enough to achieve a good level of satisfaction and aesthetic appreciation.

Allow the children to experiment with the instruments a little before you begin. Then choose a song which they like and with which they are familiar, and ask them to sing and play along with you. Depending on how many children are in the class, some might sing the song while the others play as directed by you. For this they have to watch you carefully and exercise considerable concentration and self-control. As they increase in skill and discipline, they will be able to decide for themselves when to join in and how to play.

Mindfulness throughout the day

The concept of mindfulness is implicit in all the exercises we give, and is discussed at some length in Chapter 3. It is, of course, inherent in all the exercises in this book. Mindfulness in all that one does is not an easy discipline at first, but a valuable introductory exercise, even before you have explained the concept to the children, is to stop them in what they are doing at a suitable point during the day, and ask them to resume their task with total focused awareness. For example, if the children are in the act of walking from one place to another, they can become aware of their body movements, of themselves relative to the other children and of their place in the room. They can be invited to keep up a silent running commentary on everything they are doing (e.g. 'I am walking from my desk to the bookshelf'). If the children are drawing, they can focus their awareness on the movement of the pencil on the paper, and the sensation of the pencil between their fingers. They may even hear the sound of it as it moves across the paper. They can look at the position of the drawing on the page, and so on. It is not difficult to imagine how almost anything in which the children are engaged can be broken down into different levels of awareness and sensation. Chapter 3 illustrates these kinds of activities in more detail.

The break for mindfulness might last only 20 seconds as there is usually insufficient time for it to go on much longer. Also, the activity shouldn't be so long as to disrupt the children's work. Twenty seconds a day is perfectly adequate, and the children may in any case choose to engage in the little game by themselves now and again. It can be quite fun suddenly pausing and becoming conscious of just how much information is coursing through the senses all the time. If the children wish to discuss the activity, it is useful to inform them that some people have managed to maintain this awareness for days at a time, but a few minutes now and again are a good start. Explain that the running commentary exercise does not mean that one constantly talks to oneself; it means that one is aware of every discrete activity. In the case of the children, the commentary might include 'I am hanging up my coat. Now I am walking to my seat. I am sitting down and the teacher is calling the register. Now I am getting out my reading book. I am now putting it away and now I am getting out my diary to write in it.' Obviously much will be occurring between each of these inner statements, but they are sufficient to enable the children to be deliberately aware of what they are doing, instead of being swept along by events without being sensitive to the depth and variety of their experience.

MEDITATION AT HOME

Before you begin

The introduction to working at home in the previous chapter also applies to children of this age group, so it would be useful to refer back to the pages concerned (pp. 143, 148). You will recall that emphasis was placed upon being comfortable with the activity yourself, with your relationship with your child, and with the home conditions and the place and time.

As with the school setting, the way in which you frame the exercises will influence the way in which the ideas are received by your children. Again, your knowledge of their interests and temperaments will determine how you approach things. Remember that some children take more readily to a more practical and down-to-earth approach, and have little tolerance for what they might perceive as 'way-out' notions, while other children are attracted to the unusual and the mystical. The idea of self-development with its associated benefits at school and socially will probably appeal to both types of children.

Having explained the potential benefits of the exercise and established a suitably undisturbed area for the activities, you should allow your child to ask any questions he or she might have. We give some examples of possible questions and answers on pages 139–40.

Before you begin, make sure that all those involved are sitting comfortably. Children of this age often have more difficulty than younger children in sitting cross-legged, so if they are on the floor, tell them to sit on the front part of a hard cushion so that their bottoms slope slightly forward. This automatically straightens the back. If they are using chairs, ask them to sit with their legs together and feet flat on the floor. You may advise them to put a cushion behind them. In any event, the back should be straight but not stiff and the head upright on a relaxed but straight neck. This posture is described in more detail in Chapter 6.

When the children are settled, begin with watching the

breath and counting the breath as described in Chapter 3 and elsewhere in the book. This can be followed by the other techniques described earlier in this chapter, adapted to suit your own needs.

Meditation with the whole family

All these activities can be carried out with some or all of the other family members, and may provide valuable experience in learning to share feelings with one another in safety and in being more tolerant of one another, and in simply spending more 'quality' time together. The reader can be forgiven for doubting if this works with a whole family, but it is surprising what is achievable with optimism and practice. There should be ground rules established which apply to all those present, including parents. These should be made explicit, so that the children feel a sense of equality. It might be fun to write down some of the rules together, and pin them up somewhere so that they can be referred to in the event of a dispute. Responsibility for keeping to them should be shared by all concerned.

Chapter 15

Beginning Meditation with Thirteen- to Eighteen-Year-Olds

MEDITATION IN SCHOOL

Children of this age find themselves in a very different school environment from that of their earlier school experiences. The focus is now often even less on the development of the whole child. Important examinations which can determine the child's future career dominate the ethos of the school. Work is subject- and task-orientated. And yet, these children are going through one of the most difficult periods of their lives – adolescence, that often painful and confusing period between childhood and adulthood. Hormones are unbalanced, issues of identity and belonging become of great significance, and as if that were not enough, they have to prepare themselves for those crucially important exams. It is at this age that expectations of parents and teachers become greater, and the pressure to do well increases as the anxieties of parents and teachers also increase for their own reasons.

This is often a time when children feel that they have no one to talk to about the problems which are constantly arising. Often they feel alienated from their parents since they are now more consciously aware of the generation gap, and even of their different cultures, reflected in their different appreciation of music, clothes and ways of enjoying themselves. Parents often become obstructive authority figures to the adolescent and the last people they feel they can turn to in times of need. Talking to their peers is not always possible (although this seems to be generally less of a problem for girls) because so much effort is expended in trying to 'fit in' with the group, and to be accepted and respected. Self-disclosure might 'blow their cover', and they might be seen as weak and not worthy of membership of the gang.

With so many pressures from all directions, it is not surprising that these children find it hard to relax, to work and to feel comfortable in themselves. They are on a roller-coaster of emotions, fears and hopes and they are expected to perform well in all they do.

Meditation can help these children enormously, and at this age they will be able to make very good use of it. It can help them with all aspects of life, encouraging relaxation, concentration, emotional and physical balance and self-confidence.

This chapter is shorter than the previous two which deal with the younger age groups. Working with this age group is closer in form to working with adults, particularly as the children at the upper end of this range are approaching adulthood. The earlier chapters in the book describe a wide range of meditation exercises which a teacher can use with these young people. Chapters 13 and 14, although written for the younger age groups, describe in detail several exercises which could also work very well with this age group. The children will simply do the same exercises, but at their own level.

This chapter will therefore deal mainly with the practicalities of the timetable which is less flexible than for the previous age groups. It will examine the various ways in which the subject of meditation might be introduced, both at school and at home. It will include one or two new exercises which are suitable only for this age group and case studies including one on how meditation can help sleeplessness.

Introducing the topic

As with younger children, care needs to be taken with how meditation is introduced. At adolescence, many children are very influenced by what their peers think, and may reject something to which they are secretly attracted for fear their friends might think them weird. They are often both self-conscious and image-conscious and need to be convinced that what they are doing is acceptable and that it can offer them considerable benefits. Initially, convincing them of the benefits of meditation may not be easy since there is no immediate tangible evidence, and our culture is very product-orientated. However, topic titles such as 'The Development of Human Potential' or, more directly, 'Develop your Potential', with sub-headings such as 'improve your memory', 'do better in your exams', 'increase your concentration', 'creativity and confidence' and so on, might be more acceptable than 'meditation'. You might also include a few other potential benefits, such as 'These activities can help you to be better at sport and to improve your relationships'. One idea for increasing the acceptability of meditation might be to display pictures of people that the children admire – perhaps famous sportsmen, particularly in the martial arts such as kung fu, in which the mind and body work together in perfect harmony and in conjunction with all the senses. (Chapter 4 discusses these kinds of issues in more detail.) Of course, you will have to emphasize the idea of non-aggressive use of martial arts. You may also include pictures of actors and other famous and successful people who are known to meditate and who might be role models for the children. For example, actor Richard Gere is a Buddhist who meditates regularly, and singer Tina Turner has used Mantra meditation (see Chapter 4) to help her through particularly difficult periods of her life. To arouse interest, you could perhaps include a caption such as 'What do these people share in common? Come along and see.'

Examples of cases where meditation exercises have helped children can be encouraging and you may even feel it appropriate to describe how some of the meditation practices you have done have helped you personally. Below are some accounts from young people who are currently involved in meditation activities.

Peter

Peter is eighteen years old and has sought out his own meditation class. He had heard of meditation from a martial arts teacher and since his school did not offer meditation he decided to find a class for himself. When we asked him what he thought meditation gave to him he replied, 'Oh, a lot, greater clarity of thought definitely. Your mind is totally calmed down and all your stresses and strains go away during those moments of meditation. Also I find that if your body is more relaxed, your mind isn't on the pain you might have in your leg, say, from a sports injury; you can be more in your head. You can concentrate on your work and not on your leg. In the long run, it helps with everything.

'The relaxation you get from meditation releases the stress from the muscles and the stress from emotions which have been blocked for years. You have fewer unharmonious thoughts. It's like clearing a room, sweeping away the dust. You feel happy and have a sense of well-being. You're less likely to fidget and find alternative things to do. If the whole class meditated, they would all be less likely to fidget. They'd have common goals.

'If an athlete is trying to run when he's all tensed up, it's difficult and he doesn't run very well, but if his body is relaxed, it flows and is easy. He runs faster. It's the same as the mind. If it's full of hundreds of different thoughts it can't think clearly to concentrate, but if it's clear then you can do everything better.'

Peter introduced his father to the idea of meditation and now they go to the classes together and continue the practice at home, sometimes separately and sometimes together.

Mark

At the time of writing Mark is fifteen years old and is in his first year of GCSE studies. Like Peter, he looked around for an evening meditation class since his school didn't offer one. He has been meditating regularly for just over one month. He believes that the practice of meditation has made him more focused. Before he began the classes his mind would drift off into all kinds of other places but now he experiences himself as more attentive, relaxed and confident. Describing himself before beginning mediation, he said, 'Usually little things would stress me out; now I'm not bothered by them.' He also said that his memory had improved and that his sense of well-being had considerably improved: 'I can remember lots of stuff from my childhood. I'm more cheerful. I feel fully awake in the morning, ready to face the day, and my homework is actually getting done.' He volunteered his theory of how it works for him: 'It calms the body, releases tension and discards worries, it's a way to recharge your batteries.' He concluded, 'I'm very pleased with the way meditation has improved my quality of life.'

The following case study illustrates how the relaxation and breathing exercises in particular have helped a young insomniac.

Kelly

Kelly was eighteen years old. She came to see me [Ingrid] because she was not sleeping well. She was afraid to go to sleep because she would have nightmares. This had been going on for over a year. We talked about the kinds of things which she felt were keeping her awake, and as part of dealing with her problems I introduced her to the idea of relaxation and meditation exercises. Kelly liked the idea of them from the start. Now, when she was in bed feeling anxious she would try to relax her body. Beginning with her feet, first her toes, concentrating on them one at a time, then her whole feet, ankles, lower legs, knees, upper legs, thighs, back, chest, arms, hands, fingers, shoulders, neck, face, head and so on . . .

transferring her consciousness to each part of her body until she was aware of its place on the bed, feeling the bed beneath her and the covers over her. Still physically relaxed, she would 'watch her breath' as described in Chapter 13, followed by 'counting her breath'. Thoughts which entered her head were released and allowed to float away. Kelly liked the idea of her thoughts floating away on a cloud. If she had not fallen asleep by the time she had completed this exercise, she would engage in a visualization exercise. The one she liked best was walking through a door into a tunnel at the end of which was a bright light (see Chapter 14). There she was greeted by a loving and kind person. She felt the love and peace which came from this encounter and returned slowly to the door and to her place in her bed. Soon she would fall asleep and the nightmares eventually disappeared.

You might also tell the children about the case study of Paul in Chapter 14, who found that meditation exercises helped him with his asthma, and who at seventeen years of age still finds that a short meditation (though he does not term it that), which includes the relaxation and the breathing exercises, before an examination or any disquieting situation, helps considerably.

The time and the place

Once you have the children's interest, it becomes a question of when and where to meditate. Ideally meditation should be part of the school ethos. Each session should begin and end with a minute of relaxation and meditation. This would have far-reaching effects on the work that followed. In addition to this, different kinds of meditation sessions could be arranged, but this would obviously depend on the availability of a suitable teacher who had practised meditation him or herself. For meditation to work, there must be a mutual respect between the children and their teacher.

Early morning sitting
This is a very brief sitting period which may simply take the form of sitting quietly together in a relaxing environment.

You will need to make available for at least fifteen minutes before the start of the school day a room where students can walk in quietly as they arrive, and sit with you in a circle. Soft 'New Age' music playing as they arrive, a lighted candle and an incense stick can create a very relaxing and pleasant atmosphere. For these sessions it is important that you are present, calm and relaxed, before the children arrive, while they are there and when they leave. Chapter 12 contains advice on preparing yourself quickly and simply for a meditation session. Remember that meditation and the related exercises should always be associated with calm and gentleness.

There is no need to talk to the children when they come into the meditation room, as they will quickly understand that this is a quiet time, that attendance is voluntary and that no disruptive behaviour will be tolerated. Uncooperative children will be asked to leave immediately. Remember that it is vital that the necessary permission and co-operation of school and, where appropriate, parents is obtained for work of this kind.

One way of introducing the early morning session to the children is to introduce the idea at an assembly when all are present. Make the format of the activity clear, emphasize that the sessions are optional, and that the children may walk in at any time, provided they do so quietly and without disturbing anyone, as it is a time for peace and harmony. These sessions may well be the only time that many of the children experience a relaxed and quiet environment. The sessions are an extra-curricular activity which all can attend and feel comfortable in without possessing any special skills.

If only half a dozen children choose to attend the sessions, they are still eminently worthwhile for all concerned, you included, as they allow a few moments respite from what is usually a hectic and stressful schedule.

If you have a regular group in the mornings, teach them

the relaxation and breathing techniques of 'watching the breath' and 'counting the breath'.

The room
Ideally meditation sessions should be held in a comfortable, fairly spacious room, away from a lot of noise. If students are to sit on chairs, then the chairs should be set out in a circle ready for their arrival. The students may even like the idea of bringing their own cushions to sit upon and their own special accessories, such as meditation shawls to drape around themselves while they meditate. Accessories of this kind serve to keep the body comfortable and warm while sitting, and help induce the right state of mind. Rituals such as taking off shoes on entry into the 'meditation room' are also a signal that the hurly burly of the outside world has been left behind for the time being. As suggested above, soft music, incense and a candle can transform the room you use sufficiently for its everyday associations to be lost.

When meditation sessions were held in one school early in the morning, the class using the room for their first lesson reported that the room always felt calm and peaceful on entry.

When to meditate
Besides creating a space at the beginning and end of every period, and the fifteen-minute session before school, there is little room in the fixed timetable and specialist syllabus of these older children for meditation. But Chapter 14 shows how meditation may be incorporated into many subjects in the school curriculum. Subjects such as art, English, music and drama are particularly compatible with meditation-related exercises.

Where meditation is not part of the school ethos and you are the only teacher interested in teaching it in a system where children move from room to room with different teachers for each subject, it may initially be difficult for you to reach many children. But you can still introduce your own class to the breathing exercises, and start each day with a few minutes relaxation after taking the register. Longer extra sessions can also be offered after school or at lunch time, giving you the opportunity to introduce some of the various meditation-related activities.

Explain to the children that the activity of meditation is not limited to special places and times. They can meditate anywhere, any time they feel the need, for example, when they are afraid, upset or worried. People meditate in trains, in stations, in cafés . . . almost anywhere. It helps people to reduce stress and to centre themselves.

The exercises

These can include visualizations as described in the previous chapters, particularly Chapter 13, followed by discussion and/or drawing or writing. Children of this age can derive a great deal from visualization exercises: benefits include increased calm, spirituality, creativity and insight. The following example shows how Claire, at seventeen years of age, received an unprompted insight about herself through a visualization exercise.

Claire

When Claire experienced the 'tunnel and light' meditation she found herself reluctant to move along the tunnel, saying, 'I wasn't frightened or anything and I didn't mind going through the door. I just would have preferred to stay where I was. I had to make an effort to go forward.' We asked her if she had gone to the end and had entered the light, to which she replied, 'Yes, I did and it was lovely in the light.' She asked why the person she met there had to go back. We explained that it was because she had entered another world of her own creation and that she could go back to it at any time but it wasn't usual to take it with her into everyday life. [This is something to reflect upon further.] We asked whether either of them had said anything during the encounter. Claire replied, 'Well, she spoke to me but I didn't hear anything. I didn't need to. I knew she was telling me something but I'm not sure what it was, but it was good.' Claire said that she felt more comfortable back in the tunnel, and that 'it was easier'.

Later that day, while engaged in quite a different activity unrelated to meditation, Claire suddenly said, 'I know why I wanted to stay in the tunnel now. When something new turns up I'm often reluctant to go for it. I'm like that all the time. I'm comfortable where I am. When I want something or sort of aim for something – aiming a move from A to B – instead of going for it and putting myself through the stress of getting there I look around myself where I am and make myself comfortable instead of pushing myself forward. I appreciate where I am and no longer want the thing I wanted.' During the visualization she had pushed herself into the light because we had asked her to. She admitted, 'When you asked me to be in the light I could still feel myself partly in the tunnel.' Relating back to the experience of the figure moving away from her she added, 'When I'm with friends I hate it when they walk away from me.'

You can also include mindful movement, for example the walking meditation (Chapter 7) and other concentration exercises such as 'the orange' in Chapter 13. Whatever form you decide the sessions should take, always begin with the relaxation and breathing exercises. Children in this older age range will obviously have much longer concentration spans than the younger children, so you will be able to spend longer on each of the exercises.

Relaxation exercises are described in Chapter 6. Every meditation should begin with relaxation – a focus on the body from head to foot, checking that every part is relaxed. This can be guided by talking the children through or by letting them check for themselves.

The breathing exercises of 'watching the breath' and 'counting the breath' can follow the relaxation exercise. By the end of these exercises the children will be ready to continue, either by extending the time spent on the breathing activities so that they become a complete meditation in themselves, or by sitting quietly and 'watching their thoughts', a technique briefly outlined below (p. 180). However, the breathing exercises do not come naturally to everyone and the following account illustrates some of the difficulties which may arise.

Claire (continued)

Seventeen-year-old Claire's first experiences of the breathing exercises were not without problems. She initially found these exercises both difficult and unpleasant, and had difficulties concentrating on the breath. Claire has asthma so breathing is already an issue for her. We realized that it was important for her to do the relaxation exercise first as this would induce a feeling of peace and calm, thereby reducing anxiety. We also realized that she was focusing too much on the actual process of breathing instead of simply continuing to breathe normally whilst concentrating on the awareness of the cool and warm air on the 'in' and 'out' breath respectively. This realization allowed her to improve her technique and soon she began to find it much easier; she actually enjoyed both the experience and the feeling of calm that resulted. She still did not, however, take to the 'counting the breath' exercise as she found the degree of concentration required too constraining and therefore uncomfortable. One might deduce from this that these kinds of exercise require more perseverance from asthma sufferers than people who do not normally experience breathing difficulties, but a sample of one is hardly conclusive. We decided she should focus her attention on 'watching the breath' until she felt ready to try the 'counting the breath' technique again. Besides highlighting differences between meditators this example serves to illustrate how we need to change our approach to suit the individual and not proceed relentlessly with our plan, come what may.

Watching thoughts

After the relaxation and the breathing exercises, some of the children will be able to sit quietly for quite long periods of time, remaining conscious of their breathing and watching and letting their thoughts go. Often it can be very difficult to still the mind since it seems to latch on to any external piece of information and continues to think about it. Talk to the children about the problems of stilling the mind, perhaps using the following example. If we hear an external sound, such as a dog barking, instead of just being aware of the sound and letting it go, we can see how the mind catches the thought and begins to play with it (you can refer to the analogy of the 'chattering monkey' in Chapter 1). 'Whose dog is that? Why is he barking? I wonder if he's locked up . . . People who leave their pets alone all the time shouldn't be allowed to have any . . . If I had a pet . . .' and so on. The 'chattering monkey' grabs on to thoughts and worries away at them. Explain to the children how this happens in our lives all the time. The mind turns the distracting thoughts this way and that, often allowing them to provoke strong emotions. In this way peace of mind is destroyed, and the mind runs along in an uncontrolled fashion.

Helping the children to appreciate awareness of this process is an important step towards greater mind control. Emphasize, and this is particularly important with children of this age who have for years been taught that success only comes with effort, that they should not push unwanted thoughts away, as this only leads to internal conflict. Instead, they should let them go gently and allow the next thought to come in their place, letting that go just as easily. Sometimes the image referred to earlier of thoughts floating away on a cloud or in a balloon is helpful with this. Later, when the children are much more practised, they will be able to 'watch their thoughts' without involvement.

After the breathing, the children will probably be able to meditate quietly for several minutes, allowing thoughts to enter and leave their minds gently, without becoming bound up in them. Eventually some of the older children will be able to sit in this way for up to twenty minutes or even more, thus practising meditation in its most obviously recognizable form.

Mantra meditation

This is a different form of meditation and we described it in some detail in Chapter 4. It is the repetition of a single word or phrase which can serve a number of functions, depending on the choice of mantra. It can help to keep an otherwise too active mind focused; its content can serve as an affirmation or its sound can create certain desirable mental states.

One technique for this is to say the phrase on the in-breath and to watch the space left by the phrase on the out-breath, for example, 'I create my world' as you breathe in, and observe the space as you breathe out. If the mantra is longer you would say half of it on the in-breath and the second half on the out-breath for example, 'I am healthy' on the in-breath and 'I am strong' on the out-breath. (See p. 51 for another suggestion.) Whichever type of mantra the children choose, it should be repeated throughout the meditation.

'Five minutes of life' observation

One exercise in mindfulness and concentration that older children usually enjoy is the 'Five minutes of life' observation. Ask the children to spend five minutes being totally aware of every activity they engage in, noting their senses, their feelings and reactions to everything they can, then record it as accurately as possible. An example of this which may help them to understand what to do is as follows.

> I awake; it is morning. I feel the softness of the sheets on my body. I see the ceiling of my bedroom. I feel sleepy. The ceiling is white and smooth; I am aware of a small cobweb in the corner and wonder where the spider is. Peeling back the bedclothes, I feel the cooler air and a shiver runs through me.

The carpet is soft beneath my feet; I like this feeling.
I can hear dishes being clattered downstairs and
smell coffee, a warm familiar smell. I stand up
feeling a little stiff. I stretch my whole body and feel
the pleasure of expansion. I direct myself to the
bathroom . . . etc.

MEDITATION AT HOME

Introducing the topic

Much of what was said about meditation at home for the
younger age groups also applies here. Introducing the idea to
older children is best done by leaving an interesting but
simple book on meditation lying around or by bringing it up
in normal conversation. We most of us can remember a time
in our own teenage years when we thought we were grown
up and knew everything, and were overtly dismissive of
anything our parents said. However, it is also likely that we
can remember taking in things which were being said,
although we were pretending not to listen. Later, we might
have acted upon some of these things, and pretended to
ourselves and to others that they were our ideas all along.
This is a very natural stage in growing up as children hover
between childhood and adulthood and wrestle with issues of
identity, dependence and independence. They aspire to be
adults in their own right, while secretly recognizing that they
still have a lot to learn, and that their parents might still be
able to teach them a thing or two. So don't be disheartened
if you bring the subject of meditation up in conversation and
it seems to be ignored. If your child is really against the idea,
then do not push it; he or she may come back to it later,
provided nothing is over-emphasized now. The choice is
theirs. All you can do is to provide them with the
opportunity and with your support.

However, a little planning, or at least an idea of how to
recognize and take the opportunity when it presents itself, is

often required. Maybe your child is having trouble concentrating on his or her homework or cannot think of anything to write about for an essay. Maybe he or she suffers from asthma as in the case of Paul, whom we discussed in Chapter 14. Maybe he or she is feeling stressed about impending exams, or is worrying about relationships with friends, or is generally lacking confidence. Any of these situations is a good opportunity for you to say something like, 'I've heard of some exercises which are quite fun to do and are supposed to help with these kinds of problems'. If your child is interested, you will be able to say more. If you understand your child and have read through this book, you will know how to explain more in a way that will be encouraging without suggesting pressure. Pressure only serves to produce resistance. Adolescents need to feel that they are making their own choices. If meditation is something you already practise yourself or decide to take up after reading this book, you might say, 'I've really found that meditating has helped me with all kinds of things', then elaborate on it if requested.

Meditating together or alone?

If your adolescent shows an interest in the subject, you might then find out if they would like to do it with you or on their own. Older adolescents might prefer to be given a book and read it up for themselves, whereas younger ones might welcome the time they can have you to themselves. Before you begin, you might tell them of the various options and exercises available, and let them decide which to try first. Sit down together in the recommended way, and begin the session by encouraging your child to talk about anything which might be on his or her mind. Follow this with the relaxation technique, then with the breathing techniques. If your child wishes to meditate alone, make sure a quiet room is available with no risk of disturbance. This can be a bedroom, with a note on the door saying 'meditation in progress'. Incense and soft music both aid concentration and enjoyment. Removing shoes and dressing in loose and comfortable clothing such as a track suit, or simply putting a special shawl around the shoulders, help to make meditation a special time, unlike any other. After several sessions, the act of lighting the incense stick, and putting on the music and the 'special' clothes will in themselves have a relaxing and calming effect.

Sometimes, as in the case of Peter whom we mentioned earlier in this chapter, it is the young person who introduces the topic to his or her family. It is then up to you as a parent or carer to take an interest and learn with your child. In Peter's case, he told his father about it; they now go to meditation classes together and meditate at home together twice a day.

Coping with the unexpected

On rare occasions visualization exercises can bring up unexpected experiences which you may feel unsure about handling. This is more likely to occur with the older children. Often people fall asleep during the relaxation exercise. This does not matter. There is no need to disturb them and they will usually wake naturally as the session draws to a close. Sometimes the visualization which takes them to a safe place brings tears. Cheryl, a sixteen-year-old, cried because she remembered how lovely it had been when, as a little girl, she used to sit in her grandma's loft among boxes of ripening apples and lots of old dusty toys. She had felt safe and warm. Life was not quite as cosy as that any more and she wept for the past. Many children and adults alike report reluctance to return from some visualizations, especially the 'favourite place' and the 'light at the end of the tunnel' ones (Chapters 12 and 13). Patience, kindness and understanding will help you cope with most situations which might arise during these sessions. Encourage the children to talk about the situation if they wish, but respect their need for privacy if they don't wish to share it. Always remind them that they can return to these places of beauty and safety whenever they wish. It is within their control. The strange feelings soon pass, and children learn a little more about themselves every time they happen.

A Final Note

Although this book has been written with children in mind, all the exercises are perfectly suited to adults. You can choose any level that appeals to you, and practise the various exercises for yourself.

Whatever age you are, or whatever age the children with whom you are working, all the exercises in this book can help in some way. Once learned, some of the basic meditation techniques, relaxation and watching the breath can be done anywhere at any time, from sitting in a railway station to queuing for a bus. Mindfulness should ideally be practised at all times, but even practising it now and again can serve to heighten our awareness of things around us, and of the effect we have on other people and our environment.

You will have had your specific reasons for reading this book, maybe for yourself, or more likely to introduce meditation to the children in your care. Your aims may range from helping them to improve their concentration, self-esteem, awareness and spirituality, to enhancing their creativity, imagination and social competence. Perhaps you were looking for something to help them learn to relax, thereby reducing stress. Hopefully the theory and practice described in this book go some way towards helping both you and the children to realize those aspirations.

As we have emphasized in many places, the activities described in this book are not limited to any one particular setting. We are simply exploring the potential of integrating the mind, body and spirit to create a physically and psychologically healthy and whole person with a great respect for themselves, others and all aspects of creation. The way of mindfulness and meditation is not just a practice to be fitted into spare time; it is a way of life.

It is not an easy journey, but it is an immensely rich and rewarding one, and certainly one worth persevering with. There will be times when you feel that it's not working and you may want to give up. That is a natural part of the process. Even meditation masters report that it is sometimes very difficult to meditate and remain mindful. Remember never to force meditation, but remember also that gentle persistence and perseverance are the key to success. A whole new world of experience is opening out for you and the children you teach. Reading and beginning to practise the exercises presented in this book is the first step of a long and exciting journey which you and the children in your care will share together.

A journey of 1,000 miles begins with a single step!

(Ancient Chinese Taoist saying)

Further Reading

There are many good books on meditation, although they deal with adults rather than with children, and are often written from the viewpoint of a particular spiritual tradition. However, the following suggestions will help the reader gain further relevant knowledge of meditational practices and of the psychological and physical benefits they bring.

CLEARY, J C, *Meditating with Koans*, Asian Humanities Press, 1992.
Excellent for those who wish to know more of the puzzling, intriguing, paradoxical business of meditating with Zen koans.

FERRUCCI, P, *What We May Be*, Turnstone Press, 1982.
Written from the point of view of psychosynthesis (an effective modern approach to personal growth and psychological well-being), and containing many exercises suitable for use with children.

FONTANA, D, *The Elements of Meditation*, Element Books, 1991.
Aims to provide a comprehensive all-round introduction to all aspects of the subject.

FONTANA, D, *The Meditator's Handbook*, Element Books, 1992.
Goes more deeply into the subject, looking at a wide range of techniques from different traditions, but remains non-technical and suitable for readers at all stages of experience.

GOLEMAN, D, *The Meditative Mind*, Crucible, 1989.
A good survey of the different approaches to meditation adopted by the world's great religions.

KEYES, K, *Handbook to Higher Consciousness: the Science of Happiness*, Living Love Publications, 1975.
Somewhat over-esoteric, but full of useful visualization and other exercises which can be adapted for use with children.

KORNFIELD, J, AND BREITER, P, *A Still Forest Pool*, Quest, 1987.
One of the best introductions to Buddhist meditation.

LE SHAN, L, *How to Meditate: A Guide to Self-Discovery*, Turnstone Press, 1983.
A useful practical guide, with interesting references to the relation of meditation to psychotherapy and to the paranormal.

RAM DASS, *Journey of Awakening: A Meditator's Guidebook*, Bantam Books, 1982.
Somewhat quirky, but written by an acknowledged expert.

WOOD, E, *Concentration: An Approach to Meditation*, Quest Books, 1949.
Beyond doubt the best short book ever written on the development of concentration.

Index